★
ICONS

ALCHEMY
&
MYSTICISM

THE HERMETIC CABINET

THE HERMETIC CABINET:

ALCHEMY
&
MYSTICISM

ALEXANDER ROOB

TASCHEN

KÖLN LONDON LOS ANGELES MADRID PARIS TOKYO

Illustrations: Cover: Andreas Cellarius,
Harmonia Macrocosmica, Amsterdam,
1660; Back Cover: Donum Dei, 17th cen-
tury; p. 6, from: Michael Maier; *Viatorium,*
Oppenheim, 1618; p. 6, 36, 172 from:
J. Typotius: *Symbola divina et humana,*
Prague, 1601–1603; p. 158, from: Basilius
Valentius: *Chymische Schriften,* Leipzig,
1769

To stay informed about upcoming TASCHEN titles, please
request our magazine at www.taschen.com or write to
TASCHEN America, 6671 Sunset Boulevard, Suite 1508,
USA–Los Angeles, CA 90028, Fax: +1-323-463.4442. We
will be happy to send you a free copy of our magazine
which is filled with information about all of our books.

This book also exists in an extended version:
Alchemy & Mysticism; The Hermetic Museum
ISBN 3–8228–1514-4

© 2005 TASCHEN GmbH,
Hohenzollernring 53, D–50672 Köln
www.taschen.com
© 2005 VG Bild-Kunst, Bonn, for the
illustration of Marcel Duchamp
Cover design: Sense/Net, Andy Disl &
Birgit Reber, Cologne
English translation: Shaun Whiteside, London

Printed in Italy
ISBN 3–8228–3863–2

Contents

INTRODUCTION

"It will be apparent that it is difficult
to discern which properties each thing
possesses in reality."
(Democritus, 8th century B.C.)

The hermetic cabinet

Puzzle pictures & linguistic riddles

A rich world of images has etched itself into the memory of modern man, despite the fact that it is not available in public collections, but lies hidden in old manuscripts and prints.

By imbuing them with a special hieroglyphic aura, the creators of these pictures sought to suggest the very great age of their art and to acknowledge the source of their wisdom: the patriarch of natural mysticism and alchemy, Hermes Trismegistus.

It was Greek colonists in late classical Egypt who identified their healing, winged messenger of the gods, Hermes (Lat. *Mercurius*) with the ancient Egyptian Thoth, the 'Thrice Greatest'. Thoth was the god of writing and magic, worshipped, like Hermes, as the *psychopompos*, the souls' guide through the underworld. The mythical figure of Hermes Trismegistus was also linked to a legendary pharaoh who was supposed to have taught the Egyptians all their knowledge of natural and supernatural things, including their knowledge of hieroglyphic script. The alchemists saw him as their "Moses" who had handed down the divine commandments of their art in the "emerald tablet". This *Tabula Smaragdina*, now believed to date back to the 6th-8th centuries A.D., became known to the Christian world after the 14th century through translations from the Arabic.

Also from Hermes, messenger of the gods, comes *hermeneutics*, the art of textual interpretation, and according to the author of the *Buch der Heiligen Dreifaltigkeit* (Book of the Holy Trinity, 1415), the first alchemical text in the German language, this occurs in four directions: in the natural, supernatural, divine and human sense. As used by its most distinguished representatives, alchemical literature possesses a suggestive language, rich in allegories, homophony and word-play which, often through the mediation of Jacob Böhme's theosophical works, has had a profound effect on the poetry of Romanticism (Blake, Novalis), the philosophy of German idealism (Hegel, Schelling) and on modern literature (Yeats, Joyce, Rimbaud, Breton, Artaud).

Many voices, even from within their own ranks, were raised against the "obscure idioms" of the alchemists. And their own account of their communication technique hardly sounds more encouraging: "Wherever we have spoken openly we have (actually) said nothing. But where we have written something in code and in pictures we have concealed the truth." (*Rosarium philosophorum*, Weinheim edition, 1990)

The tendency towards arcane language in "obscure speeches", in numbers and in enigmatic pictures, is explained by a profound scepticism about the expressive possibilities of literal language, subjected to Babylonian corruption, which holds the Holy Spirit fettered in its grammatical bonds. The prehistoric knowledge, the *prisca sapientia* that was revealed directly to Adam and Moses by God, and which was handed down in a long, elite chain of tradition, had to be preserved in such a way that it was protected against the abuse of the profane. To this end, Hermes Trismegistus, who, like Zoroaster, Pythagoras and Plato, was seen as a major link in this hermetic chain, developed hieroglyphs.

The Renaissance idea of Egyptian hieroglyphs took them to be a symbolic, rebus-like, esoteric script. This was influenced by the treatise of a 5th century Egyptian by the name of Horapollo, in which he provided a symbolic key to some 200 signs.

Horapollo's 'Hieroglyphica' also formed the basis for the development, in the mid-16th century, of emblems, symbols which are always connected with a short motto and generally accompanied by an explanatory commentary. They were very popular in the Baroque, and proved to be an ideal vehicle for the communication of paradoxical alchemical teaching aids and maxims.

Emphasizing their broad theoretical foundations, the alchemists often termed themselves "philosophers", describing their work simply as "art" (*ars*) or "philosophical art".

The heyday of hermetic emblems and the art of illustration coincided with the decline in "classical" alchemy, which was still capable of combining technical skills and practical experience with spiritual components. Theosophical alchemists like the Rosicrucians and practising laboratory chemists like Andreas Libavius, who sought to improve the empirical foundations of alchemy and thereby brought it closer to analytical chemistry, were already irreconcilable by the beginning of the 17th century. Although Rosicrucians did boast that "godless and accursed gold-making" was easy for them, this was a ludicrous and marginal pursuit in comparison with the main pursuit of inner purification: their gold was the spiritual gold of the theologians.

Gnosis and Neoplatonism

For the art historian Aby Warburg (1866–1929), who did pioneering interdisciplinary work in the early years of the 20th century, late classical Alexandria represented the epitome of the dark, superstitious side of man. Here, in the 1rst century A.D., in the former centre of Greek culture on Egyptian soil, with its highly diverse mixture of peoples, Greek and Roman colonists, Egyptians and Jews, the threads of all the individual disciplines making up the complex of hermetic philosophy came together: alchemy, astral magic and the Cabala. The complementary syncretic systems that nourished them, hybrids of Hellenic philosophies and oriental religions and mystery cults, are known by the two concepts of Gnosis and Neoplatonism. Both are fundamentally animistic, filled with many demonic and angelic creatures, whose power and influence determine human fate.

Gnosis means knowledge, and the Gnostics acquired this in a number of ways. The first and most fundamental form of knowledge is good news, and concerns the divine nature of one's own essence: the soul appears as a divine spark of light. The second is bad news and concerns the "terror of the situation": the spark of light is subject to the influence of external dark forces, in the exile of matter. Imprisoned within the coarse dungeon of the body, it is betrayed by the external senses; the demonic stars sully and bewitch the divine essence of one's nature in order to prevent a return to the divine home.

Under the stimulus of Zoroastrian and Platonic dualism, a painful gulf opened up between the interior and the external, between subjective and objective experience, between spirit and matter. It was cosmologically established by Aristotle (384–322 B.C.), with a strict division of the universe into the eternal, ethereal heaven and the transient sublunary sphere. This model, only slightly modified by the Alexandrian Gnostic Claudio Ptolemy (c.

A.D. 100–178), suppressed all efforts at a unified explanation of the world for two millennia.

In many Gnostic myths man is given an autonomous task of creation: in order to heal the sick organism of the world, he must lead the divine sparks of light, spiritual gold, through the seven planetary spheres of the Ptolemaic cosmos and back to their heavenly home. To the outermost sphere of Saturn corresponds the "sullied garment of the soul", the grossest material, lead. Passing through this sphere meant physical death and the putrefaction of matter that is a necessary prerequisite transformation. The subsequent stages were: Jupiter-tin, Mars-iron, Venus-copper, Mercury-quicksilver, Moon-silver and Sun-gold.

The individual metals were taken to represent various degrees of maturity or illness of the same basic material on its way to perfection, to gold. To ease its passage through the seven gates of the planetary demons, *gnosis*, the knowledge of astral magic practices, was required.

The Neoplatonists took the various diverging concepts that their master had put forward dialectically in his dialogues and poured them into the tight corset of tiered, pyramid-shaped world orders. Like a descending scale of creation, the universe overflows from the uppermost One, the good, its intervals following the harmonic laws linked with the name of the philosopher Pythagoras (6th century B.C.) and his doctrine of the music of the spheres. The inner discord of the Gnostics was unknown to them. Between the two poles of Plato's philosophy, the static and immortal world of the celestial forms and the moving and transient world of their likenesses on earth, they inserted a series of mediating authorities.

Corresponding to the tripartite division of the small world of man (*microcosm*) into body, soul and spirit was a cosmic soul which dwelled in the realm of the stars. This cosmic soul reflected the ideas of the higher, transcendental sphere of the divine intellect, and through the influence of the stars these ideas imprinted their eternal "symbols" on the lower, physical transient sphere.

Man thereby has the possibility of manipulating events in the earthly sphere, using magical practices such as the manufacture of talismans, spells and other such things to affect this middle sphere of the cosmic soul. Contact is established through the fine material of the "sidereal" or "astral body" that invisibly surrounds man. Before the Fall, according to the Gnostic-Cabalistic myths, the whole of heaven was a single human being of fine material, the giant, androgynous, primordial Adam, who is now in every human being, in the shrunken form of this invisible body, and who is waiting to be brought back to heaven. Man can communicate with the *macrocosm* through this sidereal medium, and thus receives premonitions and prophecies in dreams.

The equivalent in man of the demiurgic, world-creating drive of the outer stars is the creative capacity of the imagination, which Paracelsus calls "the inner star". Imagination is not to be confused with fantasy. The former is seen as a solar, structuring force aimed at the *eida*, the paradigmatic forms in the "real world", the latter as a lunatic delusion related to the *eidola*, the shadowy likenesses of the "apparent world".

In the Middle Ages Neoplatonism chiefly found its way into the mysticism of the Eastern Church. Although it was by no means incompatible with the rigidly hierarchical structures of the medieval state and Church, in the West it led a shadowy existence on the edge of the great scholastic theoretical structure.

But in the Renaissance the flow of Alexandrian tradition forged powerfully ahead: in 1463 Marsilio Ficino (1433–1499) translated a collection of fourteen Gnostic and Neoplatonist treatises from the early Christian period. Also attributed to the "Thrice Greatest Hermes", this collection was well-known under the title *Corpus Hermeticum*. These texts made a profound impression on the humanist intellectual world, for although they were ostensibly ancient pagan writings they still seemed to be written entirely in the tone of the New Testament, and to be imbued with the Christian spirit. Moreover, the idea of ancient Jewish teachings that reached all the way back to Moses – the Cabala – as conveyed by Picino's friend, Pico della Mirandola (1463–1494) reinforced the suspicion of a *prisca sapientia* in the Christian spirit. (In fact the Cabala, in its familiar form, was only developed out of its Alexandrian foundations in Spain and Southern France in the 12th and 13th centuries.)

The effects of Gnostic consciousness on European intellectual life are so comprehensive and omnipresent that their extent is hard to assess: the man of the *Corpus Hermeticum,* blessed with divine creative powers, merges with the image of the Renaissance man, who has begun to free himself from the bonds of the tiered, medieval cosmos and thereby moves towards the centre of the universe.

The Gnostic spark of light, which strives for divine knowledge out of the darkness of the world, is reflected in the individual Protestant soul's struggle for salvation.

Only a few alchemists were familiar with the *Corpus Hermeticum.* For them all, however, Hermes was associated with the figure who had brought them the Emerald Tablet, and with the moist, "mercurial" principle which they called the "beginning and end of the Work". The veneration of this "divine water" reached back to the upper, pneumatic waters of Gnosis which, in Greek writings from the early years of alchemy, in reference to the descent of the Gnostic Christ, flowed down into the darkness of matter to awaken the dead bodies of their metals from their slumber.

However, alchemy, as it reached Christian Europe via Spain in the 12th and 13th centuries, is much richer and more mysterious than the mystical writings of the early Alexandrian alchemists would suggest. To do justice to the "Royal Art", we might use the tripartite separation much loved by the Hermetics: according to which the part corresponding to the soul was to be found in Egyptian Alexandria. But it owes its corpus, its great wealth of practical experiences, of technical knowledge, code names, maxims and allegorical images, to its development by the Arabs. And its spirit, finally, lies within the natural philosophy of ancient Greece, where its theoretical foundations were laid in the 5th century B.C.

Concepts of natural philosophy

It is said of the philosopher and thaumaturge Empedocles that he asserted the existence of two suns. The hermetic doctrines also include a double sun, and distinguish between a bright spirit-sun, the "philosophical gold", and the dark natural sun, corresponding to "material gold". The former consists of the essential fire that is conjoined with the ether or the 'glowing air'.

Empedocles also taught that all life lay in the movement resulting from the clash between the two polar forces, love and conflict. In the *Opus Magnum* these correspond to the two alternating processes of dissolution and coagulation, disintegration and bonding, distillation and condensation. They correspond to the two polar agents of Arabic alchemy: mercury and sulphur, philosophical quicksilver and brimstone, sun and moon, white woman and red man. The climax of the Work is the moment of *conjunctio*, the conjunction of the male and female principle in the marriage of heaven and earth, of fiery spirit and watery matter (*materia* from the Latin *mater*, mother). The indestructible product of this cosmic sex act is the *lapis*, the "red son of the Sun".

In alchemy, the necessary counterforce to mercury, a force which also defines and shapes, is represented by male sulphur. Paracelsus added a further principle to the medieval doctrine of the dual principles, thereby making a decisive contribution to a more dynamic view of the natural processes.

Paracelsus identified the third fundamental principle as salt. Its property as a solid corresponds to that of the body. Sulphur, with its property of greasy, oily combustibility, mediates in the position of the soul. And mercury, the fluid principle with a propensity to sublimation, is the volatile intellect.

These Paracelsian *Tria Prima* are not chemical substances, but spiritual forces, from whose changeable proportions the invisible blacksmiths or craftsmen of nature produce the transient material compositions of the objective world. In more modern, speculative alchemy, particularly in the Masonic beliefs of the 18th century, the arcanum salt finally moved into the centre of hermetic, gnostic mysticism. Because of its curative properties it was often interpreted in Christological terms as the "coagulated light of the world", the "secret central fire" or the "salt of wisdom".

The doctrine of the four elements also goes back to Empedocles. He referred to them as the "four roots of all things": earth, water, air and fire. Hippocrates applied it as the theory of the four humours to the microcosm, and in the 4th century B.C. this theory was considerably refined by Aristotle. He traced all elements back to a common, prime matter, the *proté hyle* or *prima materia*. The alchemists also described this as "our chaos" or the "dark lump" that resulted from the fall of Lucifer and Adam. Accordingly, to sublimate it and elevate it to the *lapis* meant nothing less than bringing fallen creation back to its paradisal, primal state.

According to Aristotle, the *prima materia* conjoins with the four qualities of dryness, coldness, moisture and heat, thus developing to form the four elements. By manipulating these qualities, it was also possible, so he thought, to change the elemental combinations of materials, thereby bringing about their transmutation.

Accordingly, the work of the alchemist lies "only in the 'rotation' of the elements".

According to a law attributed to Pythagoras, quadernity defines the spectrum of all earthly possibilities. The Aristotelian fifth element, the refined "quintessence", is thus found only in the upper divine fiery heaven. It was the goal of all alchemists to bring this fifth element down to earth through the repeated transmutations that their work entailed. This meant that they would often be distilling alcohol or imagining the divine light to be within salt.

NIL SINE DEO

Macrocosm

For Plato, the universe or great world order
was created by God the creator as a manifestation
and illustration of his own perfection: "(...) and
so he formed it as a single visible living thing
which was to include all related creatures (...).
By turning it he shaped it into a sphere (...), giving
it the most perfect form of all."
(Timaeus, c. 410 BC)

Comparative depiction of cosmological systems

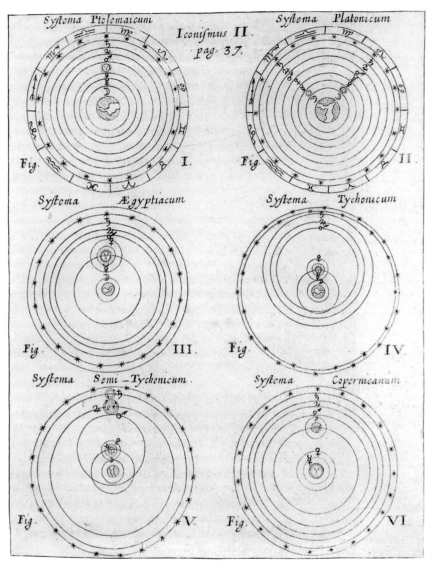

Athanasius Kircher, Iter extaticum,
Rome, 1671

Planispheric depiction of the
Ptolemaic system.

The illustration shows the Aristotelian
stratification of the four elements in the
sublunary region: the globe of the earth
consists of the heaviest and most impure
elements of earth and water, then comes
air, and finally, adjacent to the sphere
of the moon, is the lightest and purest
element, fire.

*A. Cellarius, Harmonia Macrocosmica, Ams-
terdam, 1660*

Spatial depiction of the Ptolemaic system

The outermost, opaque sphere of the fixed stars was known as the *Primum Mobile*, the "first moved", because, driven by divine love, it caused the motion of all other spheres.

A. Cellarius, Harmonia Macrocosmica, Amsterdam, 1660

"At the centre of all things resides the sun. Could we find a better place in this most beautiful of all temples, from whence this light illuminates all things at once? Rightly is it called the lamp, the spirit, the ruler of the universe. For Hermes Trismegistus it is the invisible god, Sophocles' Elektra calls it the all-seeing. Thus, the sun sits on its royal throne and guides its children, which circle it." (Copernicus, *De revolutionibus orbium caelestium*, 1543)

A. Cellarius, Harmonia Macrocosmica, Amsterdam, 1660

The World

For the Rosicrucian doctor and philosopher Robert Fludd the sun is the heart of the macrocosm. It is at the precise point of intersection of the two pyramids of light and darkness, in the 'sphere of equilibrium' of form and matter. Within it dwells the life-giving cosmic soul.

R. Fludd, Utriusque Cosmi, Vol. I, Oppenheim, 1617

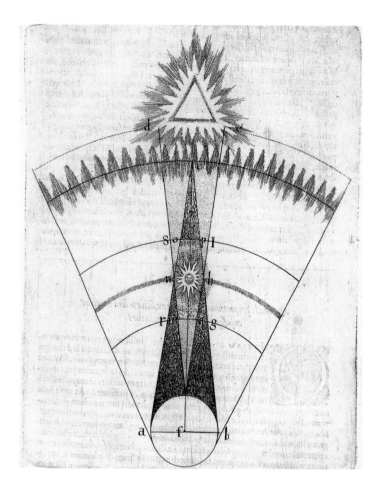

The World

In Masonic symbolism, the sun represents the imperishable spirit, immaterial gold.

A Freemason, formed from the materials of his lodge, engraving, 1754

The World

The assignment of the nine spheres to the nine Muses was the result of a harmonic vision by the Neo-Pythagorean, Martianus Capella (5th century A.D.). The scale covers a full octave.

Tragedy is assigned to the sun, comedy to the earth.

Athanasius Kircher, Ars magna lucis, Rome, 1665

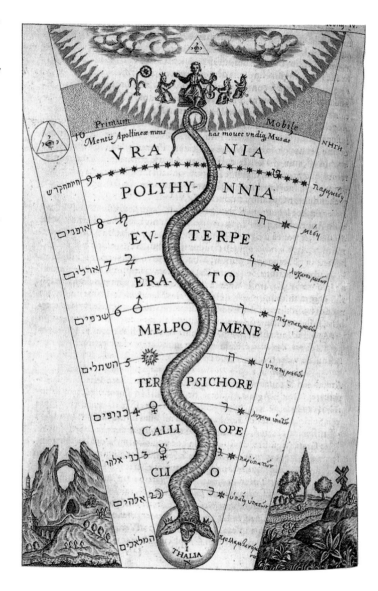

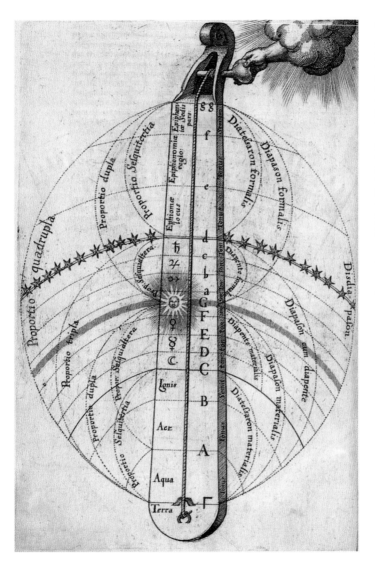

According to Fludd, "the monochord is the internal principle which, from the centre of the whole, brings about the harmony of all life in the cosmos."

By altering the tension of the strings, God, the "Great Chord", is able to determine the density of all materials between Empyreum and Earth.

Robert Fludd, Utriusque Cosmi, Vol. I, Oppenheim, 1617

Genesis

In the Tantric vision, an invisible power-point (bindu) produces the primal matter (prakriti), which consists of three qualities (gunas): sattva (essence, peace), rajas (energy, passion) and tamas (substance, inertia).

At the beginning of creation the three are in equilibrium; only their disharmony brings forth the world of diversity.

Painting, Rajasthan, c. 18th century

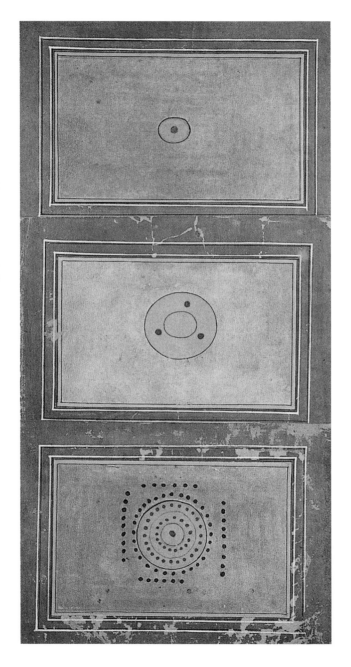

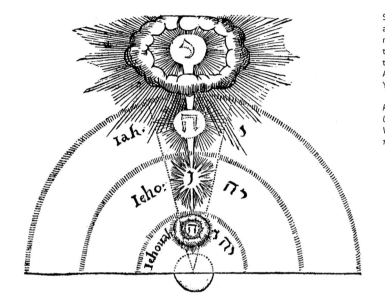

Successive utterances of the divine name produce the four worlds of the Cabala: Aziluth, Beriah, Yezirah and Assiya.

Robert Fludd, Utriusque Cosmi, Vol. II, Frankfurt, 1621

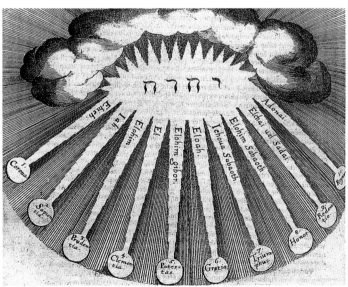

From the great tetragrammaton flow the ten "epithets" of God.

Robert Fludd, Philosophia Sacra, Frankfurt, 1626

Genesis

Light, the inexhaustible source of all things, appears in the darkness and with it the watery spirits that begin to divide into near (bright) and far (dark).

In the centre are the dark waters, far from the light, forming the source of matter; at the edge are the upper waters, from which the divine fiery heaven (Empyreum) will unfold. The bright cloud in between is a state "called variously the Earth-spirit, the Spirit of Mercury, the Ether and the Quintessence."

Robert Fludd, Utriusque Cosmi, Vol. I, Oppenheim, 1617

Genesis

The chaos of the elements from the lower waters "is a confused and undigested mass in which the four elements fight against each other."

The ideal final state of material is achieved when the elements are arranged according to the degrees of their density: (from outside to inside) Earth, Water, Air and Fire. In the centre appears the Sun, gold.

Robert Fludd, Utriusque Cosmi, Vol. I, Oppenheim, 1617

Genesis

The first day of creation:

"Let there be light!"

The dove is the spirit of God.

"The uncreated light of the spirit reflected in the sphere of the fiery firmament as in a mirror, and the reflections in their turn, are the first manifestations of created light."

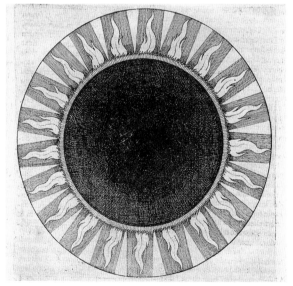

Robert Fludd, Utriusque Cosmi, Vol. I, Oppenheim, 1617

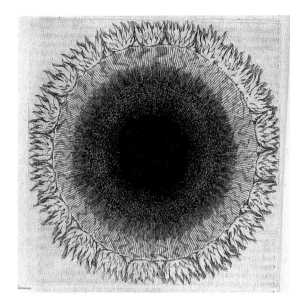

The earth belongs to the lowest level of the elements, the sediment of creation.

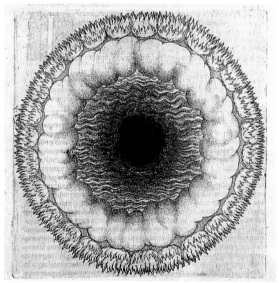

According to the proportions, the grossest element couples with the most subtle when the elements of air and water are produced.

Robert Fludd, Utriusque Cosmi, Vol. I, Oppenheim, 1617

Genesis

The second day

"And God said, Let there be a vault between the waters to separate water from water (…) And God called the vault Heaven." (Genesis 1: 6 and 8)

The ethereal sphere with the fixed stars and planets divides the upper waters (Empyreum) from the lower.

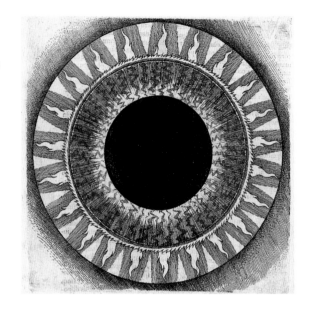

The third day

Fire arises as the first and most subtle element.

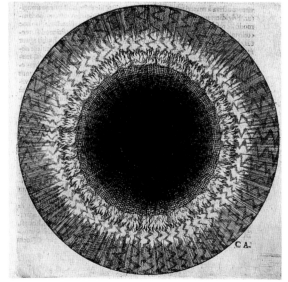

Robert Fludd, Utriusque Cosmi, Vol. I, Oppenheim, 1617

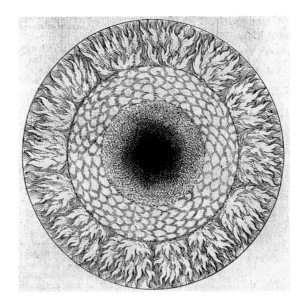

The sequence by which the elements are ordered in an ascending degree of purity – earth, water, air and fire – is repeated in the structure of the entire cosmos.

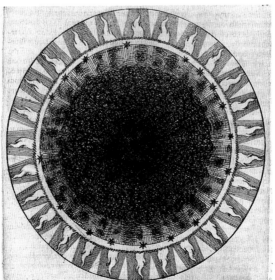

The stars on the outer edge of the ethereal sphere only became visible with the creation of the sun, for they store its light.

Robert Fludd, Utriusque Cosmi, Vol. I, Oppenheim, 1617

Genesis

"The perturbations attendant on creation had caused some of the celestial light to be trapped in the cold mass of the central earth. Obeying the law of gravity, this celestial substance began to rise towards its rightful place in the heavens, and it was thus that our sun was formed."

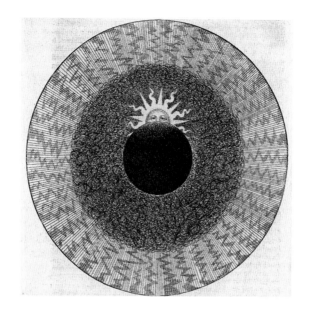

In the firmament the sun is the visible representative of the divine fire and of love. Its corresponding part in the human body is the heart.

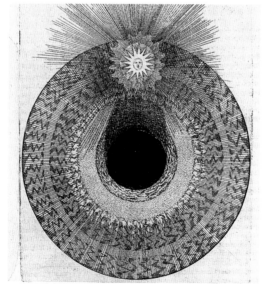

Robert Fludd, Utriusque Cosmi, Vol. I, Oppenheim, 1617

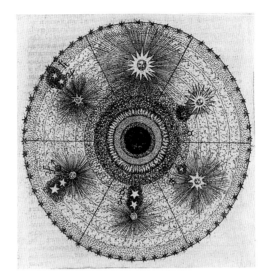

When the sinking, hot rays of the sun encounter rising, watery steam, they condense and give rise to the planets.

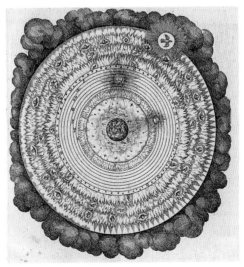

The spirit of God hovers as a dove above perfect creation, which is already menaced by the Fall.

Robert Fludd, Utriusque Cosmi, Vol. I, Oppenheim, 1617

Opus Magnum

In reference to the divine work of creation
and the plan of salvation within it, the alchemistic
process was called the 'Great Work'. In it,
a mysterious chaotic source material called
materia prima, containing opposites still
incompatible and in the most violent conflict, is
gradually guided towards a redeemed state of
perfect harmony, the healing 'Philosophers' Stone'
or *lapis philosophorum*: "First we bring together,
then we putrefy, we break down what has been
putrified, we purify the divided, we unite the
purified and harden it. In this way is One made from
man and woman."
(Büchlein vom Stein der Weisen, 1778)

The following series of illustrations is taken from the *Elementa chem-icae* of the Leiden chemistry professor J.C. Barchusen. He had them engraved from an old manuscript "to do a great favour to the adepts of gold-making". He was of the opinion that they described the production of the Philosopher's Stone "not only in better order, but also with a more correct emphasis" than anything else that he had seen hitherto.

In order to attain the lapis, the alchemist had to make a fundamental decision on which path to follow: a short "dry" path, in which the separation of the matter took place under the influence of external heat and the involvement of a secret "inner fire", and a "wet" path, which was much longer and only led to its goal through many distillations. The latter is illustrated here.

The main role in this process is played by the philosophical Mercury, not ordinary quicksilver, but a mysterious substance whose origins are entirely shrouded in darkness.

The material spirit is extracted from it. The legendary *Azoth* comes, as the agent of the Work, in the form of a dove. Like the doves that Noah sent forth to learn whether the waters had abated, it only ends its flight when the lapis is finally fixed.

Its twenty-seven-fold flight upwards and downwards here and in a related series of illustrations corresponds, in William Blake's mythology, to the flight of the twenty-seven larks, which act as bearers of conventional ideas. Only the twenty-eighth brings enlightenment and an escape from the retort's restricted field of vision. It is destroyed when the lapis is complete.

The commentaries on the individual illustrations follow the explanations provided by Barchusen.

He himself, by his own account, was never witness to a transmutation, and repeatedly declared that in all his instructions he had to rely entirely on speculation.

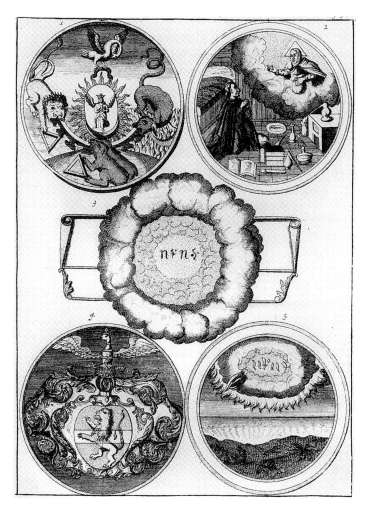

Genesis in the retort

1. The emblems of the lapis on the crescent moon. Normal gold (lion) must be twice driven by antimony (wolf) in order to lose its impurities. The dragon is philosophical quicksilver (Mercury).

2. The alchemist assures himself of God's presence in the Work.

3. Chaos.

4. The coat of arms of the lapis.

5. The four elements.

J.C. Barchusen, Elementa chemicae, Leiden, 1718

Genesis
in the retort

6. The chamois represent spirit and soul, which unite to form philosophical mercury.

7. The six planets embody the metals to which the bird mercury is related. The locked trunk says that the path to this quicksilver is hidden.

8. The inner circles are the four elements, which form the basic material of the seven metals (fixed stars).

9. Sulphur (sun) and mercury (moon), male and female.

J.C. Barchusen, Elementa chemicae, Leiden, 1718

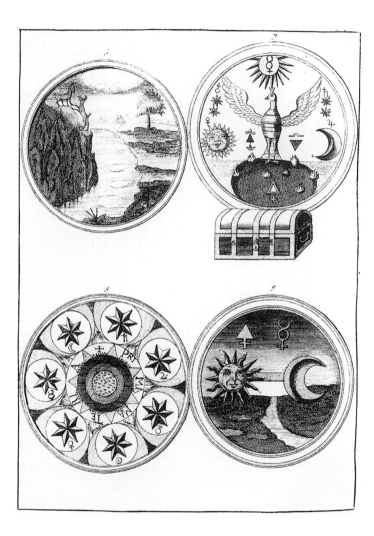

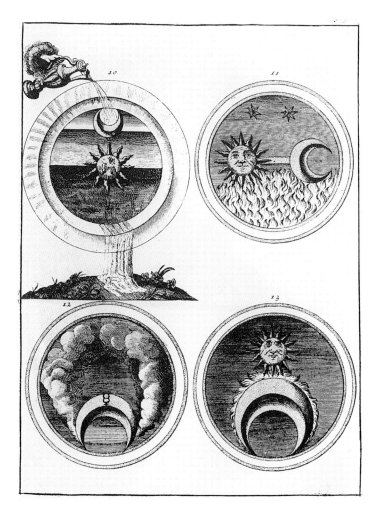

Genesis in the retort

10. Through contact with the moon and the sun, philosophical mercury attains the power of fertilizing the earth.

11. Sulphur and mercury must be freed by fire from the material which contains them.

12. Purification of philosophical mercury by sublimation.

13. Philosophical mercury is joined once more to its sulphur, so that a homogeneous liquid is produced.

J.C. Barchusen, Elementa chemicae, Leiden, 1718

Genesis
in the retort

14. Gold (lion) is purified by mixture with antimony (wolf).

15. and transformed by dissolution into philosophical sulphur

16. The furnace.

17. The retort in which sulphur and mercury are united.

J.C. Barchusen, Elementa chemicae, Leiden, 1718

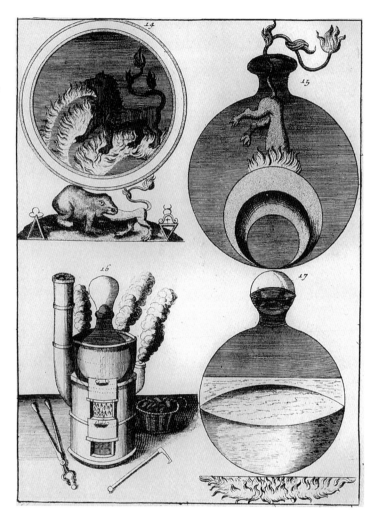

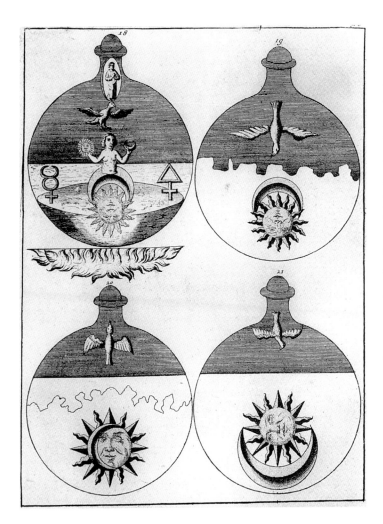

18. Philosophical quicksilver consists of liquid, mercurial components (Azoth) and solid sulphurous parts (Latona). The bird is the mercurial "spirit" that carries out the Work.

19–21. The state of putrefaction: here the four elements separate and the soul emerges from the body. The ascending bird represents the distillation of philosophical mercury. The descending bird indicates that the distillate must be repeatedly poured on to the physical residue.

J.C. Barchusen, Elementa chemicae, Leiden, 1718

Genesis
in the retort

22.–23. The blackness of putrefaction (nigredo) is purified by Azoth, the living spirit, which is extracted from the quicksilver.

24.–25. Putrefaction is the gate to the *conjunctio*, and conception. It is the key to transmutation. The star indicates that the matter is self-enclosed, and that the seeds of the seven metals lie within it.

J.C. Barchusen, Elementa chemicae, Leiden, 1718

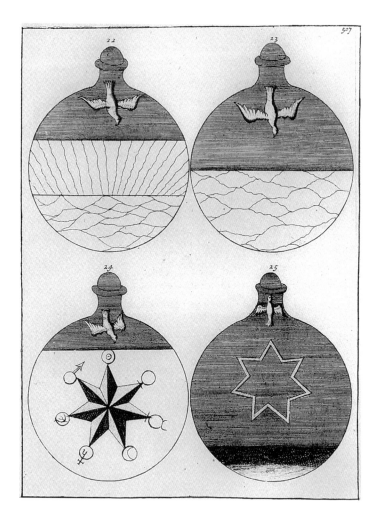

Genesis in the retort

26.–27. The black material (toad) turns white if Azoth (dove) is poured on it again. With the application of great heat, it then yields all of its liquid components.

28.–29. Under the effects of heat the elements begin to restratify.

J.C. Barchusen, Elementa chemicae, Leiden, 1718

Genesis
in the retort

31.–33. The restratification of the elements in the glass occurs by repeatedly extracting the mercurial spirit and then pouring it back.

J.C. Barchusen, Elementa chemicae, Leiden, 1718

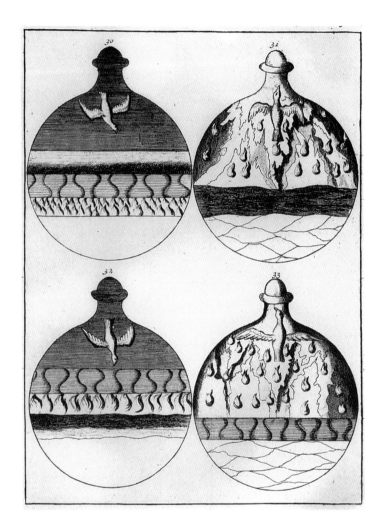

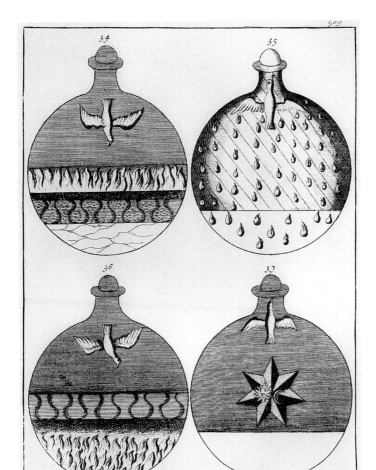

34.–36. In the seventh distillation the lapis attains its fiery nature.

37. The appearance of Apollo and Luna announces that the stone will soon have the capacity for transmutation.

J. C. Barchusen, Elementa chemicae, Leiden, 1718

Genesis in the retort

38.–41. In the ninth distillation of philosophical mercury the watery matter, followed by air, strives upwards.

J.C. Barchusen, Elementa chemicae, Leiden, 1718

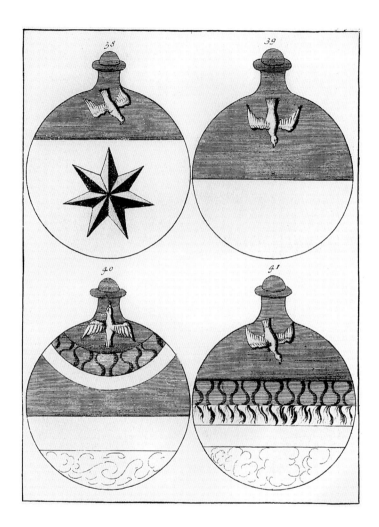

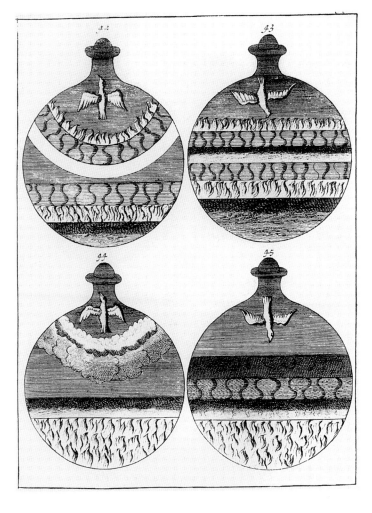

42.–45. In the
tenth distillation
and the
subsequent
moistening the
elements are
divided in two.

The fiery nature
of the *lapis* lowers
itself to the
ground. The water
turns into clouds.

*J.C. Barchusen,
Elementa chemi-
cae, Leiden, 1718*

Genesis
in the retort

46. The final sublimation of the *lapis*. Here it is represented as a pelican, said to bring its dead young (the base metals) back to life with its own blood (tincture).

47. The final solidification (*fixatio*) of the *lapis*, which rises as a phoenix in the flames.

48.–49. The elements are united and the Work completed.

J.C. Barchusen, Elementa chemicae, Leiden, 1718

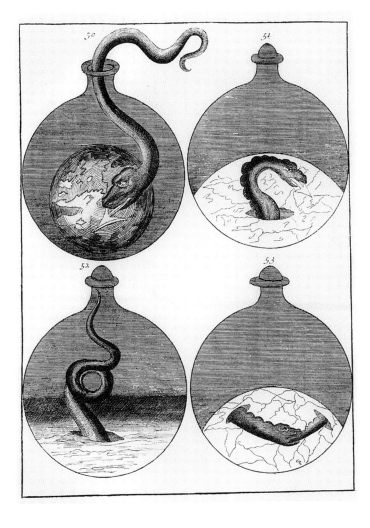

50.–53. The more transparent and subtle the consistency of the *lapis*, the higher its penetrative capacities and the greater its strength of colour. In order to intensify this, further sublimations occur: it is now fertilized with philosophical mercury (serpent), "until the serpent has swallowed its own tail" and the *lapis* is dissolved.

*J.C. Barchusen,
Elementa chemicae, Leiden, 1718*

Genesis
in the retort

The dissolution of the *lapis* (54) and the repeated distillations or sublimations (55) and subsequent moistenings (56) lead to its final resolidification (57)

J.C. Barchusen, Elementa chemicae, Leiden, 1718

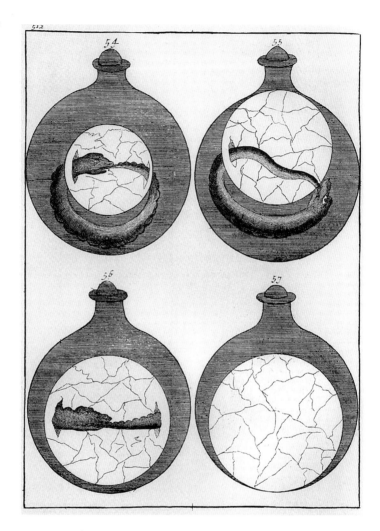

Genesis in the retort

Azoth is poured on once more (58), and the intensity of the fire is raised (59–60), for the soul must be "sweated out" (61).

J.C. Barchusen, Elementa chemicae, Leiden, 1718

Genesis
in the retort

62.–65. The *lapis* must be burned strongly and for a long time.

J.C. Barchusen, Elementa chemicae, Leiden, 1718

67.–69. The mass
is moistened
again, because the
more often the
stone is distilled
the greater is its
capacity to penet-
rate and to colour
(tincture).

*J.C. Barchusen,
Elementa chemi-
cae, Leiden, 1718*

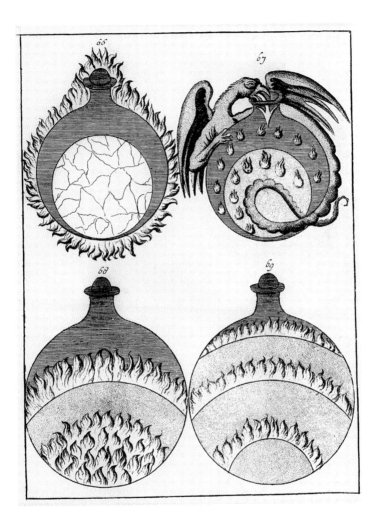

Genesis
in the retort

70.–74. In a tor-
ture by fire lasting
several days,
the stone now
matures to its
perfection and
resurrection.

*J.C. Barchusen,
Elementa chemi-
cae, Leiden, 1718*

Genesis
in the retort

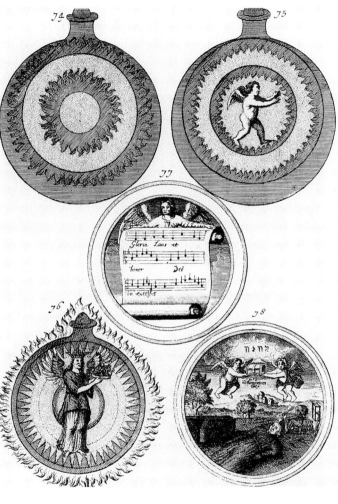

75.–78. "After much suffering and torment I was resurrected large, pure and immaculate."

Spirit and soul have now completely penetrated the body, father and son are united, transience and death have lost all their power.

J.C. Barchusen, Elementa chemicae, Leiden, 1718

Genesis
in the retort

In the Saturnine phase of the work, Mercurius fires up the "primaterial" dragon and gives it wings: that is, it begins to vaporize. The blood with which he feeds it is the universal spirit, the soul of all things.

S. Trismosin,
Splendor solis,
London,
16th century

Rebuild our diad dragon with blood, so that he may live

Genesis
in the retort

After the Saturnine restriction Jupiter promises good fortune and wealth. The phase of multiplication in the Work is assigned to him.

*S. Trismosin,
Splendor solis,
London,
16th century*

Genesis
in the retort

As the number of heads of the bird reveals, the matter has now been thrice sublimated, and is in a gaseous state. Bellicose Mars arrives.

*S. Trismosin,
Splendor solis,
London,
16th century*

The dissolved bodies are returned to true spirit.

The sun is the ruler of Leo, the sign of the zodiac, to whom, according to the inscription on the base, the matter should be thrown on the base as food.

*S. Trismosin,
Splendor solis,
London,
16th century*

Give our living dragon the wild lion to swallow.

Genesis
in the retort

Mercury arrives with two cocks, the heralds of the dawn. The pure virgin, embodying the phase of whitening (albedo), brings a happy message. Still subject to the moon and the night, she is already carrying the son of the Sun.

S. Trismosin, Splendor solis, London, 16th century

The son is born, he is greater then I.

Genesis
in the retort

Luna, who governs all things moist, gives birth to the immaculate purple-robed king: red tincture, the universal medicine that can heal all afflictions.

*S. Trismosin,
Splendor solis,
London,
16th century*

Now death is abolished and the son rules with his redness.

Genesis
in the retort

"The wind bears it in its belly."

The birth of the philosophers' stone occurs in the air.

*Michael Maier,
Atalanta fugiens,
Oppenheim, 1618*

"Its nurse is the Earth."

Mercurial water nourishes it.

*Michael Maier,
Atalanta fugiens,
Oppenheim, 1618*

Corresponding to
the four elements
(left to right:
earth, water, air
and fire) are the
four phases in the
alchemical Work
and four degrees
of fire.

*D. Stolcius von
Stolcenberg,
Viridarium
chymicum,
Frankfurt, 1624*

The source mater-
ial for the *lapis*
can be found
everywhere: in
the earth, on the
mountains, in the
air and in the nour-
ishing water.

*Michael Maier,
Atalanta fugiens,
Oppenheim, 1618*

Saturn as ruler of the two signs of the zodiac, Aquarius and Capricorn. "The ancient pagans saw Saturn not only as time,
but also as the Prima Materia of all metal
things, under whose natural-alchymistic
rule lay the truly golden age." (Heinrich
Khunrath, *Vom hylealischen Chaos,* Frankfurt edition, 1708)

De Sphaera, Italian manuscript, 15th century

Saturnine night

pag. 65.

"Behold, in Saturn a Gold lies enclosed (…). Just so man lies now, after his fall, in a great, formless, bestial, dead likeness (…) He is like the coarse stone in Saturn (…) the outer body is a stinking cadaver, because it still lives in poison."
(Jacob Böhme, *De signatura rerum*)

J. Isaak Hollandus, Hand der Philosophen (1667), Vienna edition, 1746

Saturnine
night

An allegory of the Chaos of the elements and the need to harmonize them.

Aurora consurgens, late 14th century

Saturnine night

"Take the grey wolf, the child of Saturn (..) and throw him the body of the King. And when he has swallowed him, build a big fire and throw the Wolf into it, so that he burns up, and then the King will be liberated again."

Michael Maier, Atalanta fugiens, Oppenheim, 1618

For the purification of gold (king) the impurities were alloyed with antimony, which was added to the melt. As antimony attracted and swallowed impurities, it was called the "philosophers' magnet", the "wolf of metals".

D. Stolcius v. Stolcenberg, Viridarium chymicum, Frankfurt, 1624

Saturnine
night

Trismosin tells of an angel (a code name for the mercurial components of the *Materia* which can be sublimated), which helps "a man, black as a Moor" out of an "unclean slime" (the putrefied sediment in the retort), clads him in crimson and leads him to heaven.

S. Trismosin, Splendor solis, London, 16th century

Torment
of the metals

Hermes Trismegis-
tus and the creative
fire that unites the
polarities.

*D. Stolcius von
Stolcenberg, Viri-
darium chymicum,
Frankfurt, 1624*

Solve et coagula,
dissolution and
bonding, or
mercury and
sulphur in the
image of eagle
and toad.

*D. Stolcius von
Stolcenberg,
Viridarium
chymicum,
Frankfurt, 1624*

Torment
of the metals

A symbolic representation of the three different forms of calcination of the original material.

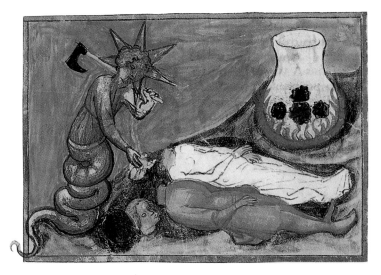

Aurora consurgens, early 15th century

The fabulous winged being represents the initial pulverization, "philosophical renewal".

Torment
of the metals

In Eleazar's inter-
pretation, the
dragon is prepared
from the philo-
sophers' vitriol
and represents the
dry path, while
Saturn-Antimony
represents the wet
path. Finally, by
achieving links to
Mercurius, both
lead to its fixing.

*Abraham Eleazar,
Uraltes chymisches
Werk, Leipzig, 1760*

"Take his soul and return it to him, for the corruption and destruction of the one thing is the birth of the other. This means: rob him of the destructive moisture and augment it with his natural moisture, which will be his completion and his life."

Aurora consurgens, early 16h century

Torment
of the metals

Son and servants ask the king for power over the realm (oro, Latin: I request; ro: anagram of French or: gold, and Hebrew: light).

The son (Azoth) kills the father.

and collects his blood.

Janus Lacinius,
Pretiosa Margarita,
Venice, 1546;
Leipzig edition,
1714

The grave (furnace) is prepared.

"Both fall through art into the grave." (QUADR: four-elemental.)

The son tries to escape, but a third comes, who has sprung from both, and holds him back.

*J. Lacinius,
Pretiosa Margarita,
Leipzig, 1714*

Torment
of the metals

In the grave "comes putrefaction in ashes or a very warm bath". (QUA: Aqua.)

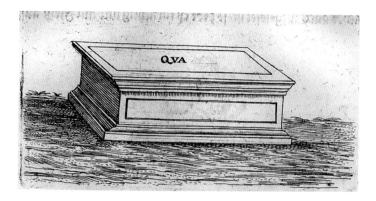

After cooling down, the result of putrefaction can be seen. (LAS : anagram of Sal.)

The bones are taken out

*J. Lacinius,
Pretiosa Margarita,
Leipzig, 1714*

Torment
of the metals

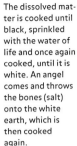

The dissolved matter is cooked until black, sprinkled with the water of life and once again cooked, until it is white. An angel comes and throws the bones (salt) onto the white earth, which is then cooked again.

The servants ask God for the return of the king.

Gradually the angels bring the rest of the bones, until the earth is completely fixed and red like a ruby. (Ro from Lat. 'ros': dew, sweat; Lat. 'rosa', the rose, a code name for tartar.)

*J. Lacinius,
Pretiosa Margarita,
Leipzig, 1714*

Torment
of the metals

The king is now
entirely spiritual

and has the power
to turn all the ser-
vants into kings.
The son is missing.
He has conjoined
with the father.

In this phase of
"projectio" (trans-
ference), the
dusty lapis is
added as an en-
zyme to the base
metals.

Janus Lacinius,
Pretiosa Margarita,
Leipzig, 1714

"Osiris is under-
handedly mur-
dered by Typhon
(*Seth*), who after-
wards scatters his
limbs, but Isis
gathers them up
and puts them
together to make
a body. But the
male member has
broken off, lost
in the water. For
sulphur perishes,
thus is sulphur
born."

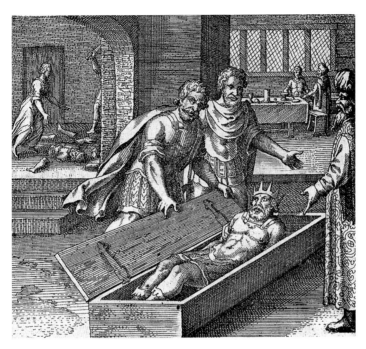

The absence of the king's male member
after he is reassembled is a reference to
the idea that the matter is now the unified
material which the philosophers call
"rebis" or "hermaphrodite".

*Michael Maier, Atalanta fugiens, Oppen-
heim, 1618*

Resurrection

The masonic lodge at the admission of a master:

A position of the Grand Master in the East

B Altar with Bible and hammer

G The old master-word on the coffin

K Tears of grief over Hiram's death

LM The burial mound with the acacia branch

O The positions of the leading officials of the lodge.

X The new recruit in the West

L'ordre des Francs-Maçons trahi...,
Amsterdam, 1745

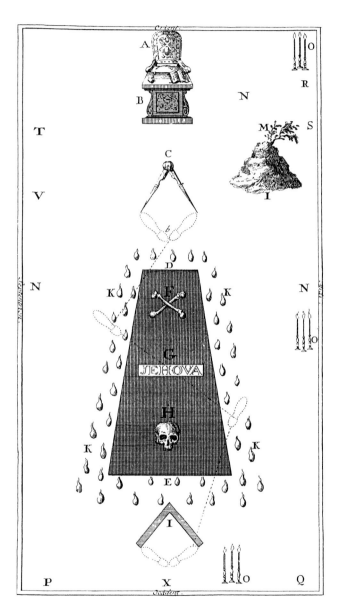

The "mosaic floor" of black and white tiles refers to the bipolar nature of earthly existence: the chimera of light and darkness, agens and patiens, form and matter. It leads to the holy of holies containing the eternal spirit-fire of Jehovah, which no mortal can see.

Work-table for the 3rd masonic degree (master), England, c. 1780

Resurrection

Sol and Luna still lie side by side as "two different things" in the glass coffin of the retort . After putrefaction they will be resurrected as "one thing from two" (Rebis).

D. Stolcius von Stolcenberg, Viridarium chymicum, Frankfurt, 1624

Without death by burning (candle) no resurrection can occur, for in ashes lies the "salt of glory"

D. Stolcius von Stolcenberg, Viridarium chymicum, Frankfurt, 1624

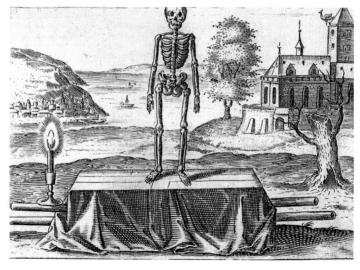

The "dark material fire" of the black sun divides spirit and soul from the putrefied body.

D. Stolcius von Stolcenberg, Viridarium chymicum, Frankfurt, 1624

"Decay is a wonderful smith", who transfers one element to the other.

D. Stolcius von Stolcenberg, Viridarium chymicum, Frankfurt, 1624

Aurora

The black sun is the outer sun, whose "dark, consuming fire" brings everything to decay. In Arabic alchemy, "the blackness or the shadow of the sun" is also a code name for the impurities of common gold, which must be washed away.

S. Trismosin,
Splendor solis,
London,
16th century

Aurora

The inner sun as an image of the *lapis*, the red-winged lion.

S. Trismosin, Splendor solis, London, 16th century

Aurora

"(...) Thus the Dawn at the peak of reddening is the end of all darkness and the banishment of night, that wintry time that one will knock against if one wanders into it and does not take care."

"Turn to me with your whole heart and do not despise me because I am black and dark, for the sun has burned me so, and the black depths have covered my face."

Aurora consurgens, late 14th century

Aurora

Runge planned the painting as part of a cycle on the four seasons as the "four dimensions of the created spirit". Morning represents "the boundless enlightenment of the universe".

Lily and dawn symbolize the rise of the age of the Holy Spirit. "

Ph. O. Runge, Der kleine Morgen, Hamburg, 1808

Aurora

"Here, two eyes have once more become one (...). By its changing gaze all things are nourished (...). If this eye closed for a moment, nothing could exist any more. For this reason it is called opened eye, upper eye, sacred eye, surveying eye, an eye that sleeps not nor slumbers, an eye that is the guard of all things, the continuous existence of all things." (*Zohar*, Cologne edition, 1982)

Little flower garden of the Seraphim, from the works of Böhme, 18th century

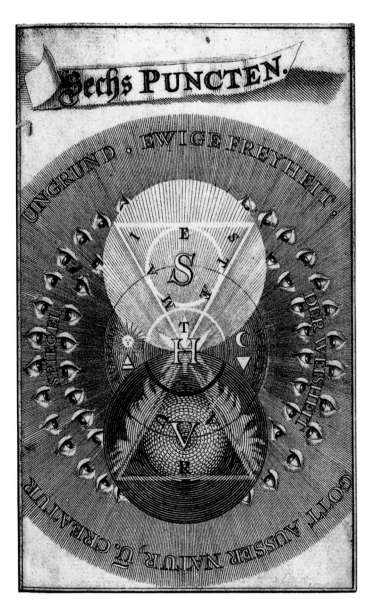

The dark background is the innermost hidden aspect of God. In a free translation of the Cabalistic *En-Sof* (the infinite), Böhme referred to him as the "unground". In the virgin mirror of wisdom, the divine will recognizes itself and "imagines from the unground in itself (...) and impregnates itself with imagination from wisdom (...) as a mother without childbirth"

*Jacob Böhme,
Theosophische
Wercke, Amsterdam, 1682*

Aurora

"The soul is an eye of fire, or a mirror of fire, wherein the Godhead has revealed itself (…). It is a hungry fire, and must have being, otherwise it becomes a dark and hungry valley."

Jacob Böhme, Theosophische Wercke, Amsterdam, 1682

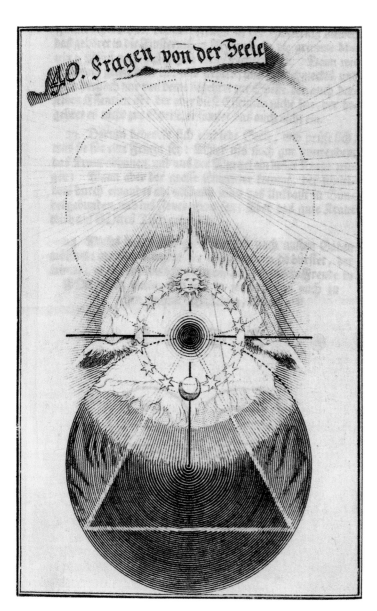

"Thus we understand the soul; that it is an awakened life from God's eye; its primal state is in fire, and fire is its life.

Jacob Böhme, Theosophische Wercke, Amsterdam, 1682

Light & Darkness

In 1600, at the age of twenty-five, according to the testimony of his pupil and biographer Abraham von Frankenberg, the shoemaker Jacob Böhme was "seized by the divine light (...) and at the sudden sight of a pewter vessel (the sweet, jovial gleam) inducted to the innermost ground or centre of secret nature".

A summary of Böhme's system:
The outermost circle "is the great Mystery of the Abyss, as the divine being in the mirror of wisdom (Sophia) gives birth to itself in the Byss". This divine procreation through the self-reflection of the original Nothing is the basic dialectical threefold step of creation.

The Name of God, ADONAI (top sphere) "indicates the opening or self-propulsion of the unground, eternal unity".

In the divine in- and exhalation of the three syllables of the Name of God JE-HO-VA, the involving principle of the wrathful father emerges as the first counterbirth: the dark world. It consists of three properties:

1. The self-centred attracting force (Saturn). From it spring astringency, hardness and cold.

2. The repellent force of "stinging bitterness", also called the "sting of sensitivity". From it emerge mercurial mobility and sensual life.

3. From the opposition of attraction and repulsion (1 + 2) results the rotating "torment of fear" (Mars).

4. Through friction and rotation, a flash is produced in the fourth property, the twofold fire of light and darkness. Finally, the third principle emerges from this, bipolar, four-elemental nature and all created life. The second exhaling principle of the son, which rises in the bright spirit-fire, consists of the properties:

5. Light or love, the true spirit (Venus).

6. Sound, tone: the joyful flow of the five senses (Jupiter).

7. The essentiality, "the Great Mystery", or the actual substance of the visible world (Luna-Sophia).

D. A. Freher, in:
Works of
J. Behmen, Law
Edition, 1764

Light & Darkness

"We have the Centrum Naturae in ourselves; If we make an angel out of ourselves, that is what we are; if we make a devil out of ourselves, that too is what we are; we are all at work, creating, we are standing in the field."
(J. Böhme)

D. A. Freher, Paradoxa Emblemata, Manuscript, 18th century

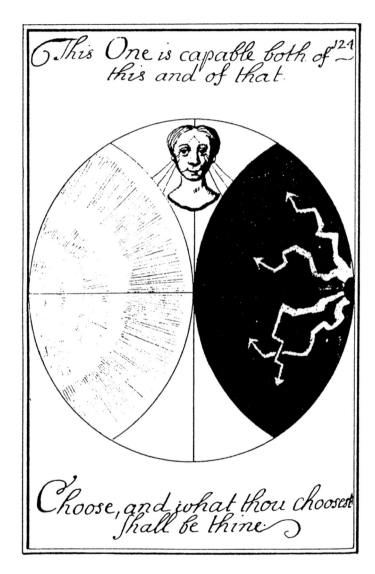

This One is capable both of this and of that. 124

Choose, and what thou choosest shall be thine.

In 1790, as an advocate of revolutionary ideals of freedom, and an opponent of all moral and state supervision, the painter and poet William Blake wrote *The Marriage of Heaven and Hell,* a spirited polemic against the traditional identification of good and evil as soul and body. "But the following (...) are true: (...) Man has no body distinct from his soul,
for that called body is a portion of soul discerned by the five senses (...). Energy is the only life and is from the body; and reason is the (...) outward circumference of energy".

The illustration refers to a vision of Böhme, in which heaven and hell are within one another, "and yet neither is apparent to the other".

The divine, fertile angels "are in the gentle water's matrix", and the hellish and infertile "are enclosed in the hard fire of anger". (Böhme)

*William Blake, The good and evil angels,
c. 1793–1794*

Light & Darkness

No. 1. Form and matter, spiritual and physical principle as a light and dark comb.

No. 2. The combs can be depicted as two hemispheres, "the upper one corresponding to the male, generative nature, and the other to the female, receptive to the seed of light.

Robert Fludd,
Utriusque Cosmi,
Oppenheim, 1619

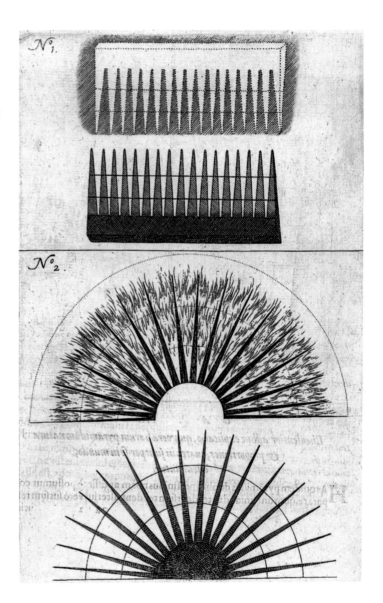

Light & Darkness

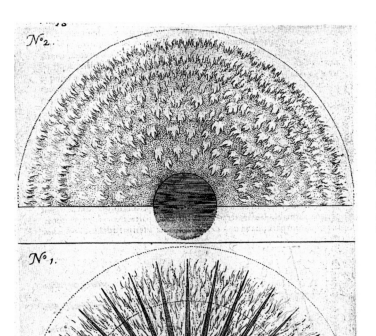

The great sex act of heaven and earth.

The divine spermatic influx is the famous dew of the alchemists, which should only be collected on spring nights, when the sky is completely clear and the temperature is mild.

Robert Fludd, Utriusque Cosmi, Oppenheim, 1619

Light & Darkness

The upper third is the region of the divine, fiery heaven (Empyran), the lower of the elemental heaven. The central sphere, which consists of equal parts of upper light and lower matter, Fludd assigned to the ether, the "fiery air". The path of the sun runs straight through the intersections, "which Platonists therefore referred to as the sphere of the soul (sol)."

Robert Fludd,
Utriusque Cosmi,
Oppenheim, 1619

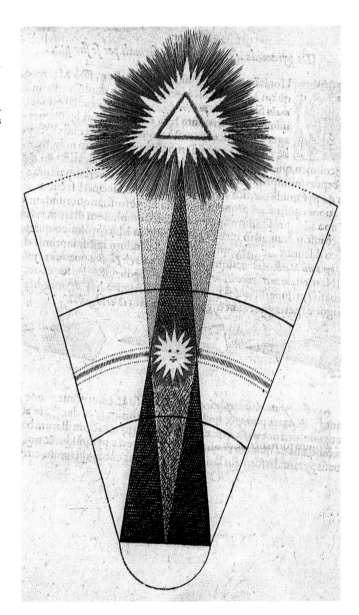

Ladder

The tree of the soul is rooted in the dark world of divine anger, and grows in two directions: to the right is self-will, to the left is self-lessness, illuminated by the light of the holy spirit. This trunk alone leads upwards through the four Cabalistic worlds or layers of the soul.

D. A. Freher, in: Works of J. Behmen, Law Edition, 1764

Ladder

The division of the upper regions of the cosmos into the nine choirs of angels is taken from the work, *On the heavenly hierarchs* by the Alexandrian Pseudo-Dionysius (c. A.D. 500).

Manuscript, 12th century

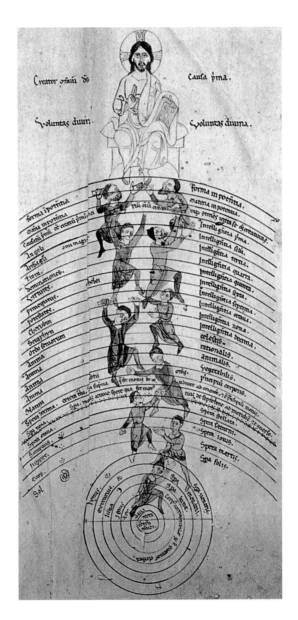

Sapientia edificauit sibi domum.

Here, the intellect stands at the foot of the ladder of creation, which leads upwards from the mineral realm via the levels of plant, animal, man and angel up to God, where Sophia, wisdom, has built her house. The figure symbolizing the intellect holds the instrument that is to enable him to climb up and down, a disc of the *ars generalis* of the Catalan philosopher and Christian mystic Ramon Lull (1235–1316).

Ramon Lull, De nova logica, 1512

Ladder

The ascent into the mysteries of Freemasonry is based on the three "Great Lights": Bible, compass and square. The Jacob's Ladder represents the process that is supposed to transform the raw stone (apprentice, *Prima Materia*) into the cubic stone (*lapis*).

The female figures: Faith, Hope and Charity. The columns: Strength (S), Wisdom (W) and Beauty (B).

J. Bowring, First Degree Board, 1819

Ladder

While the ascent on the apprentice board leads straight up a ladder – as an expression of the original will, following a projection – at the more advanced level of the journeyman, what we now have is a curved path in the form of a seven-step staircase, in which it is no longer clear where the beginning and end are.

J. Bowring, Second Degree Board, 1819

Philosophical tree

This depiction of the *Opus Magnum* is indebted to the construction of the Sephiroth tree.

The dissolving and binding powers sit opposite one another on the branches.

J. D. Mylius, Anatomia auri, Frankfurt, 1628

Philosophical tree

The Alexander novel, popular in the Middle Ages, tells of the oracular trees of the sun and moon. Observations of the appearance of tree-like crystallizations in the retort must also have contributed to the dissemination of this symbolism.

Pseudo-Lull, Alchemical Treatise, c. 1470

The Sephiroth tree is at the core of the Cabala, its most influential and multi-layered symbol. The Sephiroth are the ten, primal numbers which, in combination with the twenty-two letters of the Hebrew alphabet, represent the plan of creation of all upper and lower things. They are the ten names, attributes or powers of God, and form a pulsating organism called the "mystical face of God" or the "body of the universe". It stands on the three pillars of mercy (right), severity (left) and central balance. The central pillar forms the spine through which the divine dew flows down into the lower womb. In Creation only the effects of the seven lower Sephiroth are visible, the upper triad works outside time and beyond understanding. In the system of the four worlds it corresponds to the divine light-world (aziluth), which is separated by a veil from the two lower triads of the throne-world (beriah) and the world of angels (yezirah). The lowest Sephira, Malchut, is identified with Assia, the spiritual proto-type of the material world.

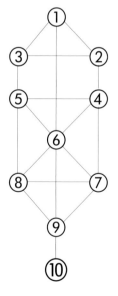

1	**Kether**	supreme crown, initial will
2	**Chochma**	wisdom, seed of all things
3	**Bina**	intelligence, upper matrix
4	**Chessed**	love, mercy, goodness
5	**Gebura**	severity, punitive power
6	**Tiphereth**	generosity, splendour, beauty
7	**Nezach**	constant endurance, victory
8	**Hod**	magnificence, majesty
9	**Jesod**	ground of all procreative powers
10	**Malkuth**	kingdom, the dwelling of God in creation

According to one doctrine of the Zohar, evil arose from an eruption of the Sephira of "severity" (5), when it was separated by a blockage of the intermediary channel from the mitigating influence of divine love (4). For the mystic Isaak Luria, this was caused by a cosmic fracture and by the fall of the lower Sephiroth, unable to bear the penetration of the upper stream of light in primal times.

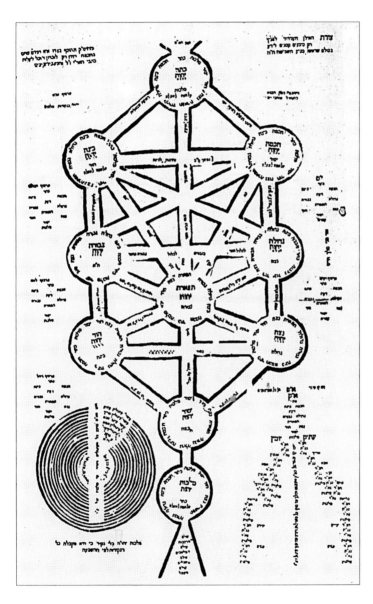

Sephiroth tree after Isaak Luria, Amsterdam, 1708

Philosophical tree

The honeycomb-like links depicted here represent new formations and restructurings of the tree after the fracture of the lower Sephiroth. Luria called the configurations "Parzufim", faces of the deity.

C. Knorr von Rosenroth, Kabbala denudata, Sulzbach, 1684

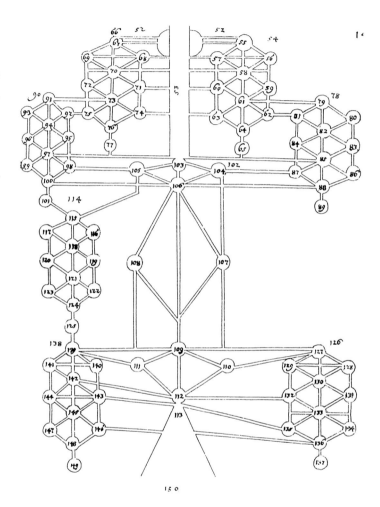

Philosophical tree

The ten Sephiroth not only form the cosmic body of the first man, Adam Cadmon, with the three upper brain-chambers and the seven limbs, but, according to the teaching of Isaak Luria, the individual Sephiroth are also reflections of his mystical face, each stressing a particular aspect.

C. Knorr von Rosenroth, Kabbala denudata, Sulzbach, 1684

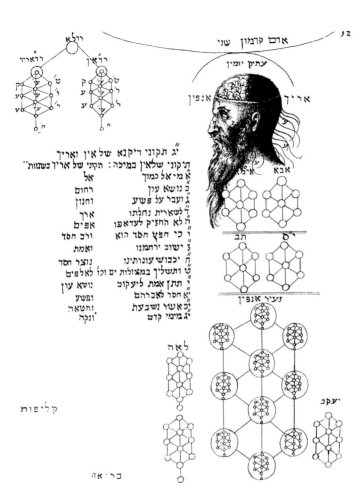

אדם קדמון שני

עתיק יומין

אריך

אנפין

"יג תקוני דיקנא של אין ו.אריך

תיקוני שלאין במיכה : תקוני של אריך בשמות"

אל אָ מי·אל כמוך

רחום ב נושא עון

וחנון ג ועבר על פשע

ארך ד לשארית נחלתו

אפים ה לא החזיק לעדואפו

ורב חסד ו כי חפץ חסד הוא

ואמת ז ישוב ירחמנו

נוצר חסד ח יכבוש עונותינו

ל אלפים ט ותשליך במצולות ים וכו'

נושא עון י תתן אמת ליעקוב

ופשע יא חסד לאברהם

וחטאה יב אשר נשבעת

ונקה יג מימי קדם

אבא

תב ס"ג

צעיר אנפין

לאה

קליפות

יעקב

בריאה

Philosophical tree

According to the law of the Pythagorean Tetractys, the four seeds of the arcane name of God unfold on ten levels.

Manuscript, Salonica

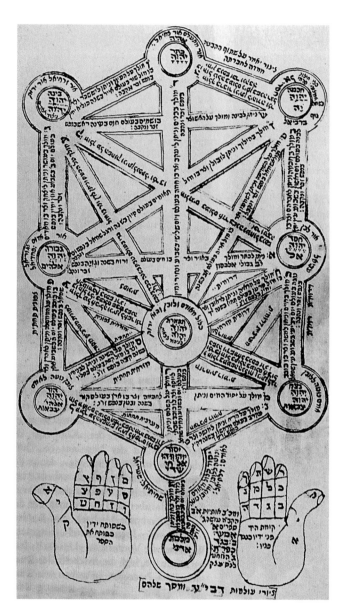

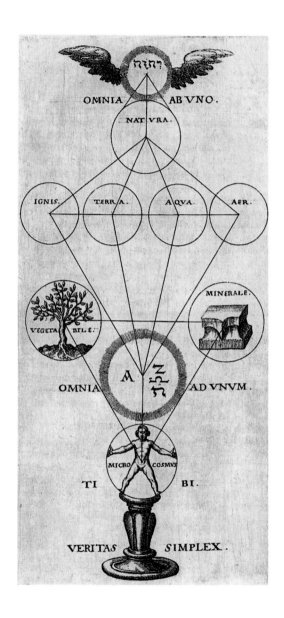

Philosophical tree

The "Tree of Pansophia" was the name that the Rosicrucian Daniel Mögling from Constance (alias Theophilius Schweighart) gave to his diagram, in which the harmonic connection of microcosm and macrocosm is to be contemplated.

Theophilius Schweighart, Speculum sophicum Rhodo-stauroticum, 1604

Heinrich Khunrath's "Whole circle-round
(...) stage of eternal wisdom" is filled with
the spiritual salt of wisdom, the "Tartarus
Mundi" or "central salt-point of the great
building of the whole world" into which all
the spatial lines of Hans Vredeman de
Vries' perspectival construction vanish.

*Heinrich Khunrath, Amphitheatrum
sapientiae aeternae, 1602*

Like bees attracted by the scent of the
rose, the lovers of Theo-Sophia stream by
from all directions to climb the seven
steps of the "mystic ladder," through "the
gate of eternal wisdom".

*Heinrich Khunrath, Amphitheatrum
sapientiae aeternae, 1602*

Mandala

Inscription above the emblem: "God is the fortress of all who believe in him"

Inscription beneath the emblem: "We trust in God when the flood begins"

M.J. Ebermeier, Sinnbilder von der Hoffnung, Tübingen, 1653

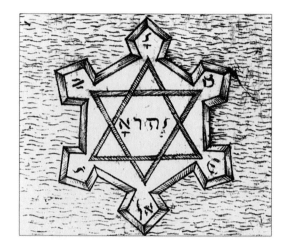

On the art of warfare and the planning of fortifications.

Robert Fludd, Utriusque Cosmi, Vol. II, Oppenheim, 1619

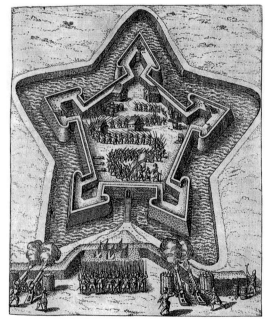

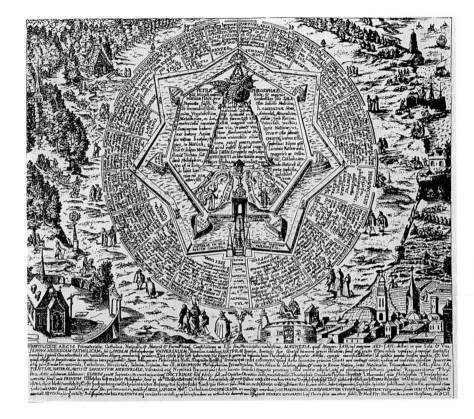

Twenty-one paths lead to the alchemistic fortress but only on one, the enthusiastic path of the fear of God and of prayer, can it be entered. This path alone brings the knowledge of the correct source material. The seven corner-points of the fortress are the seven phases which lead to the central rock of the *lapis*. Here is the throne of "our Mercury", the dragon, "who marries himself and impregnates himself."

Heinrich Khunrath, Amphitheatrum sapientiae aeternae, 1602

Mandala

This Tibetan mandala palace is divided, analogous to man as the divine measure of all things, into the three
levels of body, language and spirit, to which, in this *Mandala of the Time-Wheel*, precisely 722 Tibetan deities are assigned.

Kalachakra Mandala, gouache, Tibet, 18th century

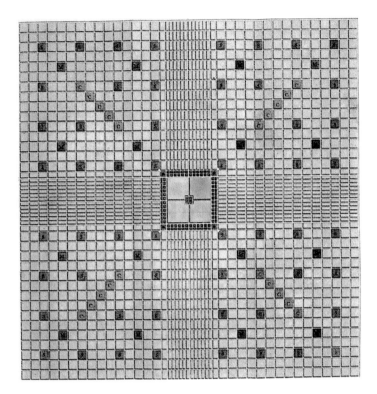

As in Blake's poems, in the writings of his contemporary, Richard Brothers, democratic convictions mingle with Biblical tradition and the author's own visionary experience. He identified the fallen Jerusalem with the London of his own time. Brothers based his detailed map of the city on the descriptions of the prophet Ezekiel.

Engraving by Wilson Lowry, in:
R. Brothers, A Description of Jerusalem,
1801

Dew

"Blessed of the
Lord be his land,
for the precious
things of heaven,
for the dew (...)".
(Deuteronomy
33: 13)

"Our dew, our
matter, is celes-
tial, spermatic,
dewish, electric,
virginal, univer-
sal." (From the
writing of Count
Marsciano, 1744)

*De alchimia,
Leyden, 1526*

Plate 4

From the Mutus Liber (mute book), published in La Rochelle in 1677. The alchemical work was here depicted in a series of 15 plates. The alchemical couple as the lower correspondence to the sun and moon in the harvesting of the dew, which must occur in the months of April (Aries) and May (Taurus).

Dew

Plate 6

The result of the forty-day digestion and a second distillation is the appearance of a fixed sulphurous blossom called the "philosophers' gold".

Plate 7

The result of the distillations is conjoined with the extract that has been concentrated by the secret, lunar fire. At the bottom, Antimony-Saturn devours the child or the "philosophers' sulphur". After being purified, it is brought to whitening (Diana).

Dew

Plate 11

The philosophical Mercury now appears elevated to purple redness.

Dew

Plate 12

Filled with inner dynamism, the sulphur-bull bucks and the dew in the bowls vibrates, sated with the nitric heavenly spirit, pure salt-petre.

Dew

Plate 13

The sulphurous blossom has turned into a small sun, which has the power to take the philosophical Mercury to its highest stage of consistency.

Plate 15

The alchemical couple celebrate the coming of the dawn. The pagan Hercules has completed the deeds of the Work, and remains as a physical residue on the floor, while, thanks to the dew (the roses), his incorruptible spirit body rises into the air.

Serpent

"Sow the gold in the white, foliate earth which is the third earth that serves the gold, it tinges the elixir and the elixir tinges it in turn."

Aurora consurgens, early 16th century

Sourdough is a favourite image of the ferment used in the process to raise the matter.

Aurora consurgens, late 14th century

"The supreme serpent (No. 3) is the cosmic spirit which brings everything to life, which also kills everything and takes all the figures of nature. To summarize: he is everything, and also nothing."

It is called *Ouroboros*. In Coptic *Ouro* means king, and in Hebrew *ob* means a serpent.

Abraham Eleazar, Donum Dei, Erfurt, 1735

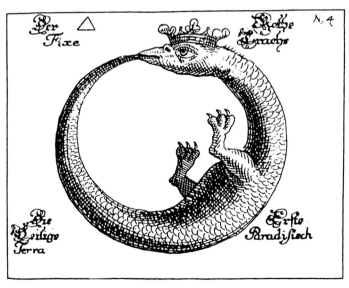

Serpent

"These are the two snakes fastened around Mercury's staff, with which he demonstrates his great power and changes into whichever forms he wishes (…)."

Livre des figures hieroglyphiques, Paris, 17th century

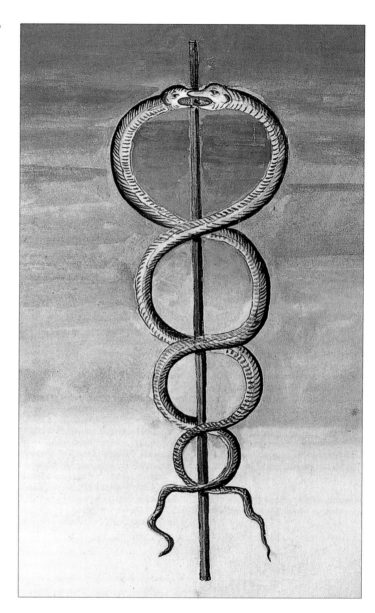

Allegory of the marriage of the dual principles in the work: on the left the female, mercurial side with the pelican as a symbolic animal, and on the right, the male, sulphur side with the fire-bird, the Phoenix.

Figuarum Aegyptiorum Secretarum, 18th century

Serpent

The "Mercurial tail-eater" is "our subject". "From this one root will sprout roses, the supreme good." The white rose signifies the lunar "Philosophical Tincture", the red rose the solar "Metallic Tincture". The mysterious "blue rose" in the middle is called the "flower of wisdom".

Hieronymus Reussner, Pandora, Basle, 1588

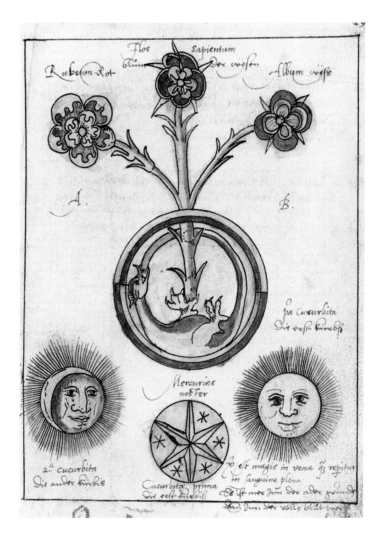

Serpent

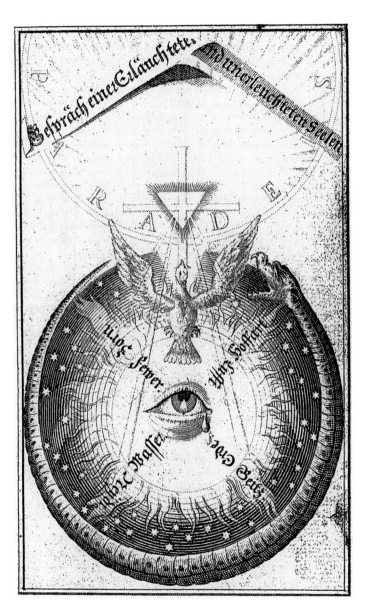

Since Vulcan lit the mercurial wheel of anguish into which the soul had imagined itself, "its meaning only stands after the multiplicity of natural things". It is entirely subject to the changeable play of the passions.

The illuminated soul counsels the poor soul to break the bonds of the monstrous snakehusk by introducing it to Christ.

Jacob Böhme, Theosophische Wercke, Amsterdam, 1682

OPUS MAGNUM: Serpent   **133**

Serpent

The "Red Sea" in the caption above this detail from the Ripley Scroll was a well-known code name for the divine mercurial water and its tincturing power.

Ripley Scroll, manuscript, 16th century

Joel 2, 13: "Rend your heart, and not your garments, and turn unto the Lord, your God."

The fiery soul has entered a false shelter with fire, and must break out again with fire and violence, or the diabolical serpent or the astral world spirit will keep it in its prison.

J. Böhme, Weg zu Christo, 1730 edition

Conjunctio

"Our Mercurial dragon" can only be conquered by Sol and Luna together, that is, in order to kill him one must remove his sulphur and lunar moisture at the same time.

Aurora consurgens, early 16th century

"It is said: Woman dissolves man, and he makes her solid. That is: The spirit dissolves the body and makes it soft, and the body fixes the spirit."

"Senior says: I am a hot and dry Sol and you Luna are cold and moist. When we couple and come together (...) I will with flattery take your soul from you". *(Aurora consurgens)*

Aurora consurgens, early 16th century

The king, Gabricius, and his sister, Beya, want to embrace "to conceive a son whose like is unknown to the world".

J. D. Mylius,
Anatomia auri,
Frankfurt, 1628

Conjunctio

The royal pair
seeks to unite to
give birth to a son,
a king "his head
red, his eyes black,
his feet white: this
is mastery".

Donum Dei,
17th century

F. SOLVTIO PERFECTA III.

"Return the nature of the four elements, and soon you will find what you seek, but to return nature means making corpses into spirits in our mastery."

*Donum Dei,
17th century*

Conjunctio

FERMENTATION

"But here Sol is enclosed and poured over with 'Mercurio philosophorum'."

Rosarium philosophorum, 1550

MULTIPLICATION

"Here, the water sinks/

And gives the earth its water to drink again."

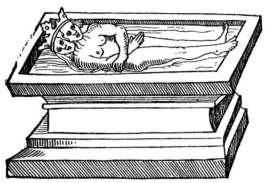

REVIVAL

"Here the soul comes from the sky, fine and clear.

And resurrects the philosopher's daughter."

All illustrations: Rosarium philosophorum, 1550

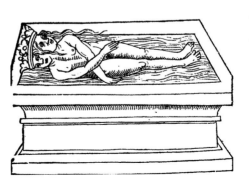

Androgyny

After purification by fire and the dissolution of their bodies in the mercurial bath, the royal brother and sister are united. The ravens indicate the stage of putrefaction.

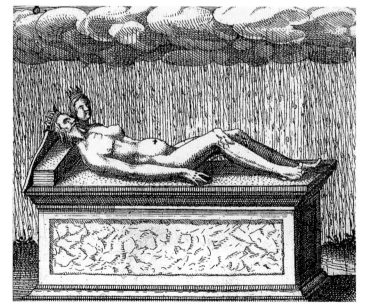

The pair arise as a rebis from the grave of putrefaction, and are cleaned of their blackness by the dew of heaven.

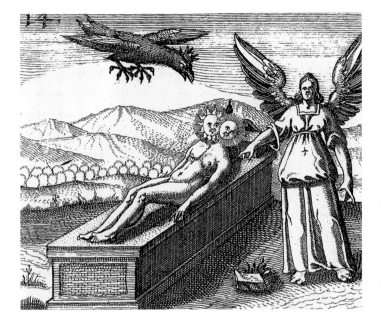

Philosophical gold and silver appear on the faces of the rebis. The presence of the two winged creatures indicates the final processes of sublimation.

The pelican, feeding its young with its blood, symbolizes the final phase of the Multiplicatio.

All illustrations: D. Stolcius von Stolcenberg, Viridarium chymicum, Frankfurt, 1624

Androgyny

"The hermaphrod-
ite, lying in the
dark like a corpse,
needs fire."

The philosophers
call the cold and
moist matter,
woman (moon),
the hot and dry,
man (sun). The an-
drogynous being is
all four qualities
at once.

*Michael Maier,
Atalanta fugiens,
Oppenheim, 1618*

Right:
William Blake,
Jerusalem,
1804–1820

Androgyny

Here, the south wind a symbol of the totaly of sublimations is represented as a large eagle, gradually uniting the two opposites. The three legs on which the androgynous being stands, refer to the three-footed stand on which the retort is exposed to the fire.

Aurora consurgens, Early 16th century

Androgyny

This androgynous being is the spectral, immodest nature from "Lucifer Anti-Christ and his mother: one body and soul, fixed and volatile. Herein consist the natural arts of this world".

Buch der Heiligen Dreifaltigkeit, 15th century

Androgyny

"Make of man and woman a circle, from that a square, then a triangle, then another circle, and you will have the philosophers' stone."

Michael Maier, Atalanta fugiens, Oppen-heim, 1618

According to Tantric doctrine, the final truth consists in the complete interpenetration of Shiva and Shakti, of male and female energy. Shiva, the upward-pointing triangle, represents the static aspect of the supreme reality; Shakti, the downward-pointing triangle, represents the kinetic energy of the objective universe.

Vajravarahi Mandala, Tibet, 19th century

Androgyny

In the first Work the saturnine source material is sublimated thrice by being moistened with the 'boy's urine', a well-known code name for the mercurial water.

After the conclusion of the third and last Work the elixir has the power to penetrate all impure metals.

Androgyny

There are three Works in the *Opus Magnum*. The philosophers speak of three bowls and three degrees of fixation, indicated here by the three arrows.

Worldly power falls to its knees before the glory of the 'red son of the sun'.

All illustrations: Speculum veritatis, 17th century

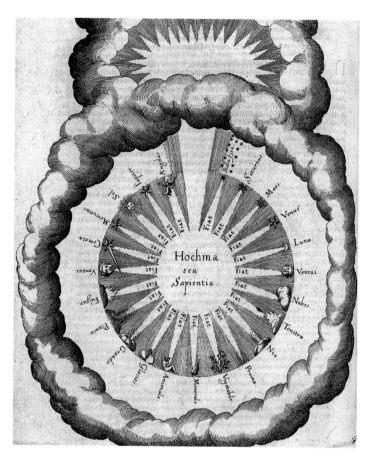

In this illustration, Fludd followed the interpretation of Genesis in the first book of the Zohar, which provides a description of the way in which, in the concealed depths of the divine unground, there first forms a fog, from which a spring then erupts. In this, the primal point, lights up. The Cabalists identified this primal point as the wisdom of God, his "Sophia". It corresponds to the second Sefira Chochma or Hochma.

Robert Fludd, Philosophia Sacra, Frankfurt, 1626

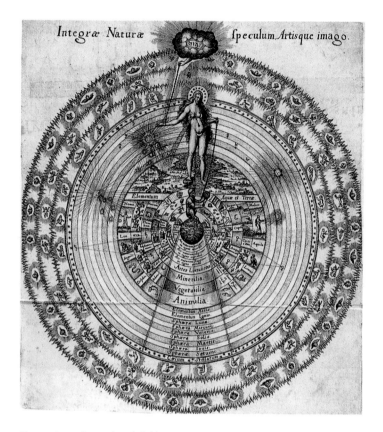

Nature, the nursing mother of all things, connects the divine fiery heaven, the astral, ethereal heaven and the sublunary, elemental world. She is the "soul of the world", the mediator between the divine spirit and material expression. "

Robert Fludd, Utriusque Cosmi, Vol. I, Oppenheim, 1617

Matrix

Nature advises the "aimlessly wandering alchemist" to leave the narrow circle of mechanical laboratory chymistry.

Miniature painting by Jehan Perréal, painter at the court of Margaretha of Austria, 1516

The honouring of Sophia as the mystical bride of the philosophers or 'mistress of the inner world', often intersects with worship of the divine Mercurial water.

Hieronymus Reussner, Pandora, Basle, 1582

In the view of Böhmes pupil Abraham von Franckenberg, all illnesses are based on false, self-centred imaginings, which poison the astral body (the "mummy"), and thus pollute the blood. The whole balance of the elements in the body is thereby finally destroyed.

Three kinds of medicine were available: the Cabalistic, from the spirit and the word of Christ, the magical in the meditation of the healing serpent, and the Chymical, with wine and oil.

Abraham von Franckenberg, Raphael oder Arzt-Engel, 1639 (reprinted, 1925)

Matrix

Mary and Jesus are one substance which is embodied in a condensed, solid state by the mother, and in a dissolved, spiritual state by the son. The sun symbolizes God the Father and the twelve stars the elements in the three forms of appearance, "of the spirit (son), of the soul (father) and of the corpse (mother)".

Buch der Heiligen Dreifaltigkeit, early 15th century

Microcosm

"The world is primarily the totality of everything,
consisting of heaven and earth (...).
In the second mystical sense, however,
it is appropriately identified as man.
For, as the world has grown out of four elements,
so does man consist of four humours (...)."
(Isidore of Seville, A.D. 560–636, De natura rerum)

Human Form Divine

The frontpiece to
the first volume of
Utriusque Cosmi
shows, in the
outer circle, the
Ptolemaic macro-
cosm, whose re-
flection in all parts
is man.

*Robert Fludd,
Utriusque Cosmi,
Vol. I, Oppenheim,
1617*

Human Form Divine

The last visions of
Hildegard von
Bingen, written
down in 1163–1173,
concern the in-
volvement of man
in the order of
God's creation.
The divine love of
the son appears
to her as a red,
cosmic figure in
the sky, dwarfed
only by the good-
ness of the Father.

*Hildegard von
Bingen, Liber
Divinorum Operum,
13th century*

Human Form Divine

In the pre-Aryan Indian tradition of Jainism, cosmic man is not an immaterial God-figure, but the organism of the world itself. This anthropomorphic cosmos "never had a beginning and will never end.

The form and dimensions of the cosmic primal man, Gujarat, 17th century

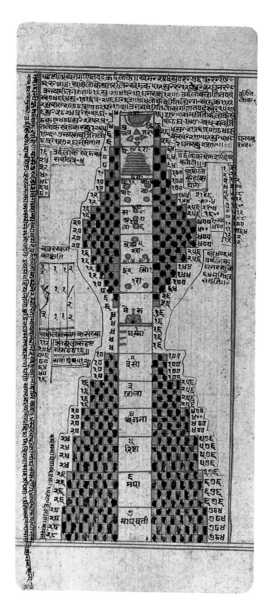

Human Form Divine

"For all are Men in Eternity, Rivers, Mountains, Cities, Villages / All are Human, & when you enter into their Bosoms you walk / In Heavens & Earths, as in your own Bosom you bear your Heaven / And Earth & all you behold; tho' it appears Without, it is Within, / In your Imagination (William Blake, *Jerusalem*)

William Blake, The Sun at its Eastern Gate, c. 1815

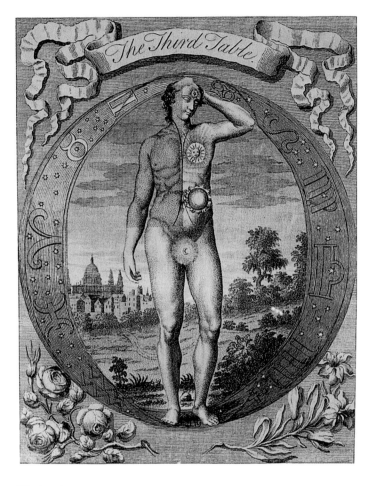

"Man is made of all the forces of God, of all seven spirits of God. (...) But because he is now corrupt, the divine birth does not always swell within him. (...) For the Holy Ghost cannot be grasped and fixed in sinful flesh; but it ascends like a lightning flash (...)" (J. Böhme, *Aurora*) The ascent of this "salnitric fire-crack" through the seven source-spirits has often been compared to the awakening of the snake-fire, the *kundalini* in Hindu yoga, which rises through the seven delicate centres of the body, the chakras, above the head, where it dissolves into pure knowledge.

D. A. Freher, in: Works of J. Behmen, Law edition, 1764

In his *Theosophia practica* (1696) Böhme's pupil Georg Gichtel described how the wheel of the planets lies on the body in seven diabolical seals.

Georg Gichtel, Theosophia practica, 1898 edition

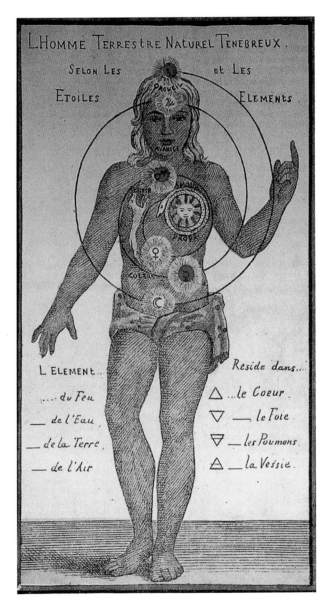

Human Form Divine

The cosmic spirit linking ody and soul is represented as the string of a microcosmic, monochord. At birth, the soul descends along the marked intervals from the higher spheres in man and in death it rises back along them.

Robert Fludd,
Utriusque Cosmi,
Vol. II,
Oppenheim, 1619

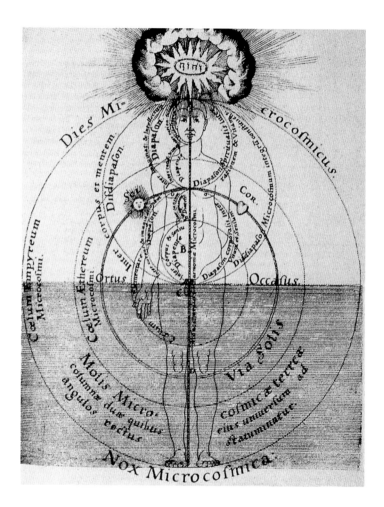

The twelve signs
of the zodiac and
their influence on
the parts of the
body.

*Hebrew
manuscript,
14th century*

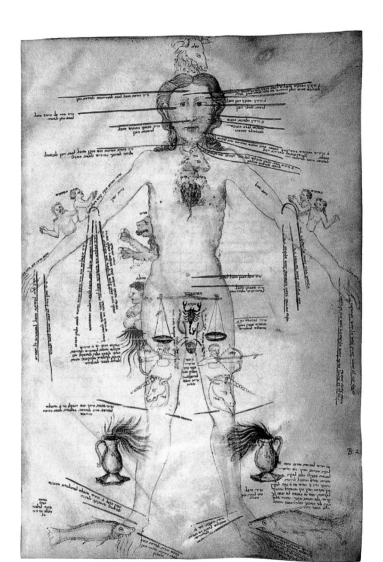

Signatures

a. Brow of a peace-loving and successful man.

b. Brow of a spiritual man with an inclination towards the priesthood.

c. Brow of a man who will die a violent death.

d. Brow of a successful soldier.

e. Brow of a man threatened by an injury to the head.

f. Brow of a poisoner.

From: H. Cardanus, Metoposcopia, Paris, 1658

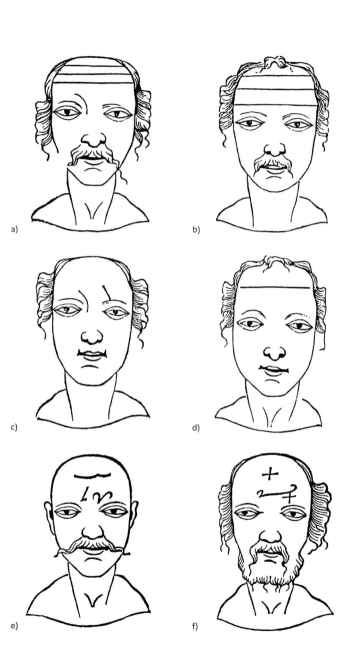

a)

b)

c)

d)

e)

f)

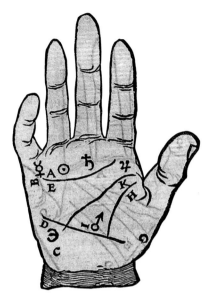

A Imperfect table line

B Sister of the lifeline

C Line of the liver and the stomach

D Sister of the nature line

E Lifeline

Johannes ab Indagine, Introductiones Apostelesmaticae, 1556

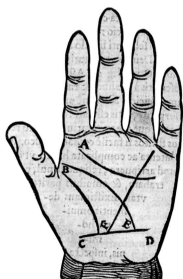

A Line of table or fate

B Line of life or of the heart

E Central nature line

F Line of liver or of the stomach

Johannes ab Indagine, Introductiones Apostelesmaticae, 1556

Signatures

According to della Porta, the whole natural world consists of a network of secret correspondences which can be revealed through analogy. A plant leaf in the shape of a set of deer's antlers is related to the character of that animal. People who look like donkeys are stupid; Those who look like oxen are stubborn, lazy and easily irritated.

Giambattista della Porta, De Humana Physiognomia, 1650

The heavenly alphabet of the southern hemisphere

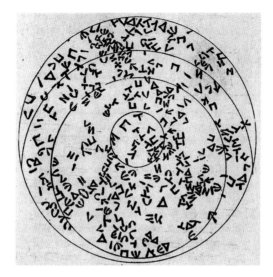

"In the wide space of heaven (…) are figures and signs with which one can discover the deepest secrets. They are formed by the constellations and stars (…) These brilliant figures are the letters with which the Holy and Glorious One created heaven and earth (…)." (Zohar)

Karl von Eckhartshausen, Aufschlüsse zur Magie, Munich, 1788

The heavenly alphabet of the northern hemisphere

Rotation

"The essence of God is like a wheel (...),
the more one looks at the wheel,
the more one learns about its shape,
and the more one learns,
the greater pleasure one has in the wheel (...)."
(J. Böhme, 1612)

Wheel

The microcosm at the intersection of the compass points, with the four main and eight subsidiary winds. The main winds correspond to the four humours.

Astronomical manuscript, Bavaria, 12th century

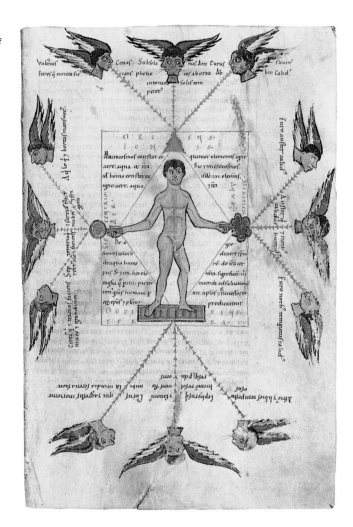

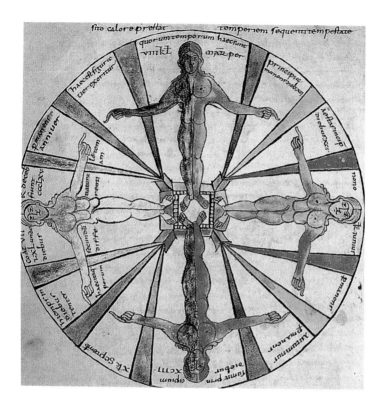

The four figures represent the seasons in
the wheel of the twelve months. Their
microcosmic equivalents are the four
humours. Autumn corresponds to black
gall (Melancholia – Earth), summer to
yellow gall (Cholera – Fire), spring to the
sanguine (Air) and winter to the phleg-
matic humour (Water).

*Isidore of Seville, De natura rerum,
manuscript, 9th century*

Wheel

The properties of
the seven planets
or 'source spirits'
in Böhme's sys-
tem.

Jacob Böhme,
Theosophische
Wercke,
Amsterdam, 1682

Through the circulatory transformation of the elements and humours, the opposites are united and matter passes from its temporary, heterogeneous state into a permanent, homogeneous state.

L. Thurneysser, Quinta essentia, 1574

Wheel

The basic powers of man in the Indian symbol of the team of horses:

"The self (atma, the divine core of being) owns the chariot, the body is the chariot, intuitive distinction and recognition is the charioteer; the function of thought is the reins; the powers of the senses are the horses; and the objects or spheres of sensory perception are the track. Man, in whom are combined the self and the powers of the senses and of thought, is called the eater or the enjoyer."
(Katha Upanishad, 8–6th century B.C.)

Bhaktivedanta Book Trust, 1987

In William Blake's mythology, the zoas are
the "four Mighty Ones in every Man",
they embody his "eternal senses", and
their four faces look in the
direction of all four worlds.

Wheel

Representation of Ulmannus' correspondence system, which influenced Böhme's mythology.

Buch der Heiligen Dreifaltigkeit, early 15th century

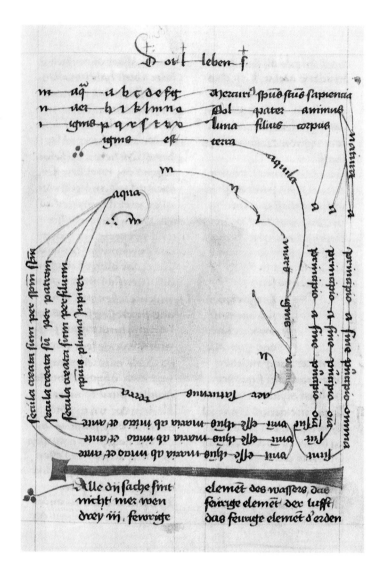

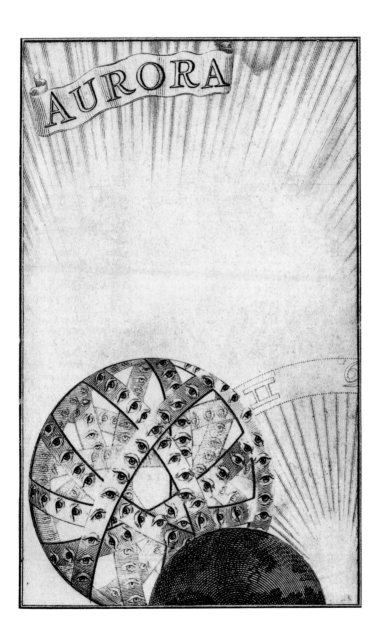

"If I should describe to you the godhead (...) in the greatest depth, it is thus: as if a wheel stood before you with seven wheels, one made into the other (...)."

Jacob Böhme, Theosophische Wercke, Amsterdam, 1682

Wheel

From the 'Centrum Naturae', the salnitric cross-ground, there emerges in various degrees of the mixture of fire and water the mystery of colours.
1. Blue: entity
2. Red: father in the brilliance of fire
3. Green: life
4. Yellow; son
5. White: brilliance of God's majesty as a quintessence.

Jacob Böhme, Theosophische Wercke, Amsterdam, 1682

Cadmus, the serbent-slayer, who embod-
ies the fixing properties of sulphur, is seen
here giving the philosophical colour-wheel
its first rotation.

Speculum veritatis, 17th century

Wheel

Influenced by Jacob Böhme's writings, which the writer Ludwig Tieck had recommended to him in 1801, P. O. Runge began to develop his own mystical colour theory, which he applied in all his painting.

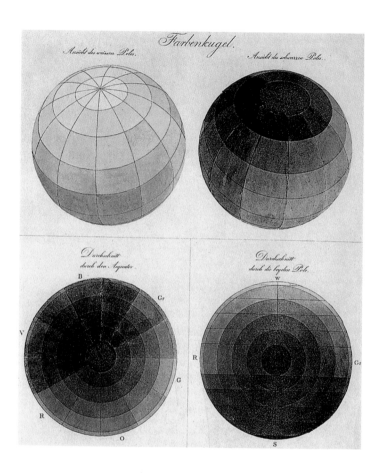

Goethe, who built on the mystical colour-theories of the alchemists, tried to connect the qualities of colours as experienced by the senses with ethical categories. Here he assigns the four spiritual capacities of man to the six colours of his circle.

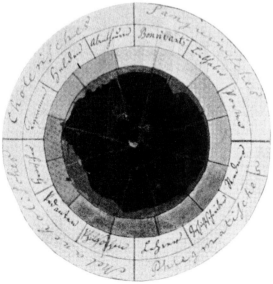

On this "rose of the humours", a collaboration between Goethe and Schiller in 1799, the four humours of man are assigned to Goethe's colour circle.

In alchemy, the white and the red rose are
well-known symbols for the lunar and the
solar tincture, from which the "precious
rose-coloured blood" of Christ-Lapis
flows.

*RobertFludd, Summum Bonum, Frankfurt,
1629*

The evening before Easter an angel gives the legendary founder of the Rosicrucian order, Christian Rosencreutz, an invitation to the mystical wedding of bride and bridegroom. With a blood-red sash hung across his white apron, and with four red roses on his hat, he sets off the following day.

Johann Valentin Andreä, Die Alchemische Hochzeit von Christian Rosenkreuz (1616), Ed. J. van Rijckenborgh, 1967

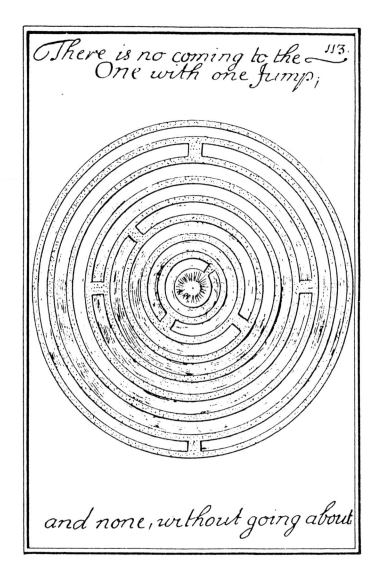

There is no coming to the **113**.
One with one Jump;

and none, without going about

The soul of the
Christian pilgrim is
guided by the
word of God.

*Hermann Hugo,
Gottselige
Begierde,
Augsburg, 1622*

Pilgrim

William Blake developed a special reversed process for etching, which is continually reflected in his writing: the spaces which are etched away are "the transient individual conditions", which disappear in the purifying fires of the last Judgement. What remains are the "eternal lineaments", the "signatures of all things".

Pilgrim

"Let us leave theories there and return to here's hear." (James Joyce, *Finnegans Wake*)

Marcel Duchamp, Door as a substitute for two doors, Paris, 1927

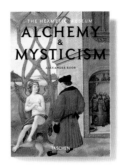

Alchemy & Mysticism
The Hermetic Museum /
Alexander Roob / Flexi-cover,
Klotz, 712 pp. / € 19.99/
$ 29.99 / £ 14.99 / ¥ 3.900

Encyclopaedia Anatomica
Museo La Specola Florence /
Flexi-cover, Klotz, 712 pp. /
€ 19.99/ $ 29.99 / £ 14.99/
¥ 3.900

"These books are beautiful objects, well-designed and lucid." —*Le Monde,* Paris, on the ICONS series

"Buy them all and add some pleasure to your life."

Alchemy & Mysticism
Alexander Roob

All-American Ads 40ˢ
Ed. Jim Heimann

All-American Ads 50ˢ
Ed. Jim Heimann

All-American Ads 60ˢ
Ed. Jim Heimann

Angels
Gilles Néret

Architecture Now!
Ed. Philip Jodidio

Art Now
Eds. Burkhard Riemschneider,
Uta Grosenick

Berlin Style
Ed. Angelika Taschen

Chairs
Charlotte & Peter Fiell

Design of the 20ᵗʰ Century
Charlotte & Peter Fiell

Design for the 21ˢᵗ Century
Charlotte & Peter Fiell

Devils
Gilles Néret

Digital Beauties
Ed. Julius Wiedemann

Robert Doisneau
Ed. Jean-Claude Gautrand

East German Design
Ralf Ulrich / Photos: Ernst
Hedler

Egypt Style
Ed. Angelika Taschen

M.C. Escher

Fashion
Ed. The Kyoto Costume
Institute

HR Giger
HR Giger

Grand Tour
Harry Seidler,
Ed. Peter Gössel

Graphic Design
Ed. Charlotte & Peter Fiell

Havana Style
Ed. Angelika Taschen

Homo Art
Gilles Néret

Hot Rods
Ed. Coco Shinomiya

Hula
Ed. Jim Heimann

India Bazaar
Samantha Harrison,
Bari Kumar

Industrial Design
Charlotte & Peter Fiell

Japanese Beauties
Ed. Alex Gross

Kitchen Kitsch
Ed. Jim Heimann

Krazy Kids' Food
Eds. Steve Roden,
Dan Goodsell

Las Vegas
Ed. Jim Heimann

Mexicana
Ed. Jim Heimann

Mexico Style
Ed. Angelika Taschen

Morocco Style
Ed. Angelika Taschen

**Extra/Ordinary Objects,
Vol. I**
Ed. Colors Magazine

**Extra/Ordinary Objects,
Vol. II**
Ed. Colors Magazine

Paris Style
Ed. Angelika Taschen

Penguin
Frans Lanting

20ᵗʰ Century Photography
Museum Ludwig Cologne

Pin-Ups
Ed. Burkhard Riemschneider

Provence Style
Ed. Angelika Taschen

Pussycats
Gilles Néret

Safari Style
Ed. Angelika Taschen

Seaside Style
Ed. Angelika Taschen

Albertus Seba. Butterflies
Irmgard Müsch

**Albertus Seba. Shells &
Corals**
Irmgard Müsch

Starck
Ed Mae Cooper, Pierre Doze,
Elisabeth Laville

Surfing
Ed. Jim Heimann

Sydney Style
Ed. Angelika Taschen

Tattoos
Ed. Henk Schiffmacher

Tiffany
Jacob Baal-Teshuva

Tiki Style
Sven Kirsten

Tuscany Style
Ed. Angelika Taschen

Women Artists
in the 20ᵗʰ and 21ˢᵗ Century
Ed. Uta Grosenick

ICONS